Setting Up Running Charity Shops

An *Essential* Guide

by

John Tough

Published by the Association of Charity Shops

Printed with the support of Propress Steamers.

"We love fabric"

© Association of Charity Shops
Central House, 14 Upper Woburn Place, London WC1H 0AE

Company No. 3709512

VAT Reg. No. 731 3311 79

First published 2006

Printed by Lamport Gilbert Limited
3 Darwin Close, Reading, Berkshire RG2 0TB

Cover photos reproduced by kind permission of
Helen and Douglas House Hospice, Minds Matter,
Oxfam GB and Shelter Trading Ltd.

British Library Cataloguing in Publication Data.

A catalogue record for this book is available from the British
Library.

ISBN 0-9553376-0-7   **(10 digit)**

ISBN 978-0-9553376-0-4   **(13 digit)**

Foreword

With over 7,000 charity shops in the UK, the charity retail sector is a thriving and efficient source of income generation and a great platform for raising public awareness for hundreds of good causes.

However, setting up and running a successful charity shop isn't as easy as it sounds. There are many issues to consider. Site selection, volunteer management, stock generation, marketing and security all present challenges for the uninitiated. Whilst there are many parallels with commercial retailing, operating a profitable and commercial charity retail business requires knowledge and skills that have until now remained in the heads of charity retailers.

This book solves the problem - it provides up-to-date guidance and acts as an information source for anyone interested in our sector. As the organisation supporting and promoting good practice and high standards in charity retailing, the Association of Charity Shops is delighted to have persuaded John Tough to write it. With over 30 years of work in charity retailing, he has a wealth of experience and knowledge, which can now be passed on.

This book is an invaluable guide not only for those thinking about opening their first charity shop but also as a training and education resource for existing charity shop managers. It also imparts useful information for members of trustee boards with little knowledge of charity retailing and is a valuable information resource for those working to advise or provide services to the sector.

We are sure you will find this book informative, accessible and highly readable.

Stephen Robertson
Chairman
Association of Charity Shops

Acknowledgements

There are many people who have assisted me in writing this book – but first and foremost I should acknowledge Lekha Klouda who had the confidence in me to suggest that I write it in the first place! Furthermore, I am grateful to Lekha, her staff and the directors of the Association for their guidance on some of the more technical content as well as the endless proofreading. I should also like to thank Heather Messam, a former colleague at the British Red Cross, who contributed substantially to the section on marketing. Thanks are due also to *Charity Finance* magazine for allowing us to include many of the performance statistics from their 2004/5 annual charity shops' survey.

Finally, I cannot fail to mention the hundreds of charity shop staff and volunteers I have had the privilege to work with over the past thirty-five years – much of what I have shared in this book has been learnt from them and particularly during those exciting pioneering days I spent at The Spastics Society during the 1970s and 1980s.

John Tough

Table of Contents

1

Overview of Charity Shops

A Brief History

Although charity shops are to be found in a number of countries including Scandinavia, the USA and Australasia, they are predominantly a UK phenomenon with this country probably setting the standard for the rest of the world to follow.

Since Victorian times, there has been a tradition in the UK of raising funds through church bazaars, bring and buy sales and jumble sales etc. so the charity shop is simply a permanent representation of a long-established fundraising concept.

Whilst in the UK we refer to these shops as charity shops, the same concept in other English speaking countries may be known as Gift Shops or Opportunity Shops; the latter usually abbreviated to "Op Shops"

Although the Salvation Army has operated shops since the latter part of the nineteenth century and the British Red Cross since the 1940s, the development of charity shops occurred mainly after the Second World War when in 1947, the Oxford Committee for Famine Relief (Oxfam) opened its first shop to help women and children in Greece. This was followed in the succeeding decades by most of the larger charities setting up chains in their own right with development being particularly rapid in the late 1970s and 1980s.

Charity shops are now a feature of practically every high street. Exactly how many there are is not recorded. However, the 2004-5 annual survey published by *Charity Finance* includes data from 5,815 shops. By adding in an estimate for the shops that did not contribute to the survey, there may be a total of 7,500 shops.

Accepting this estimate, and applying the survey's average income per shop of £1,581 per week, we can calculate an estimated annual income for UK charity shops of £617m. Hence, the sector is, by any standards, a significant activity attracting 2.2% of the national retail clothing and textiles spend of *£27.9b and a saturation of, on average, one charity shop per 8000 of population.

(* *Source: National Statistics, Retail Sales 2000.*)

Evolution

The development of charity shops has come a long way since the pioneering days of the 1970/80s. A charity shop in the early days would typically have been lent by a sympathetic landlord on a temporary rent-free basis prior to sale or letting. Essential features of these shops would have been:

- Run entirely by volunteers
- Reliant on stock donations brought directly through the door
- Set up on a shoe-string budget using a hotchpotch of display equipment usually scrounged from neighbouring shops
- Unheated and dimly lit
- A biscuit tin serving as a cash register
- No pre-pricing of stock with price negotiated at the counter
- No stock rotation
- Little regard for selecting only the best items for sale
- Prevailing and extremely off-putting aroma of damp old clothes
- An abundance of untested electrical items and other potentially dangerous items on sale
- Limited trading hours – usually 10.00am – 4.00pm for five days per week.

Nevertheless, these primitive shops, because of their low operating costs, were usually extremely profitable returning a net contribution of well over 50%. After all, there were no salaries, stock collection costs or rent to pay!

As the years progressed, many charity chains sought the security of permanent occupancy rather than the uncertain duration of temporary albeit, rent–free occupation. Additionally, charities were becoming concerned about the effect that their down-at-heel shops were having on the national image of the parent charity. However, because of the poor image of these early shops, attempts by charities to acquire leases were often thwarted by landlords' reluctance to accept charities as leasehold tenants.

It was time to 'clean up the act' and become more professional by introducing higher retail standards more in keeping with commercial shops. Additionally, it was recognised that a more attractive and inviting appearance would entice a proportion of the shopping public who had hitherto been put off by the seedy image.

Over the succeeding decades the following significant innovations evolved:

- Leasehold and even freehold occupancy
- Professional shopfits with attractive display lighting
- Pre-pricing of goods
- A system of stock rotation
- Trained and salaried staff
- Improved cash control via cash registers
- House-to-house stock collections – bag drops
- Extended trading hours
- Compliance with Health and Safety legislation and trading standards meaning that many potentially harmful stock items were prohibited from sale
- A more selective approach to the items deemed fit for sale
- Introduction of bought-in goods ranges to supplement donated stock
- Efforts to keep the shops smelling sweet!

Progress has been such that amongst most sectors of the community it is now socially acceptable to purchase and wear used clothing. Indeed, rather than conceal the fact that an admired outfit has been purchased at a charity shop, a satisfied customer will often proudly declare its origin and bargain price.

Whilst these initiatives undoubtedly improved overall profitability, the downside was that year-on-year the margin of profit was reduced, resulting in a current average net contribution for the sector of just 20%. However, as a higher profit in pounds is more useful to charities than a higher percentage profit, it would seem that increased professionalism, despite its incumbent costs, has been the right way to evolve. When challenged by a Finance Director on reducing margins, one perhaps over-protective manager of charity shops was reported to have responded: "Well, what would you rather have, increased percentages or increased pounds?"

The Conversion Process

In essence, **a charity shop's function is to convert gifts-in-kind into cash**. The majority of charities (except those providing clothing and other items directly for overseas aid) would obviously prefer to receive the cash directly without suffering the time-consuming and expensive process of converting one into the other. With sector costs currently running at 80%, the costs of the conversion process consumes most of the value of the gift-in-kind donation.

An analogy here is the cost of extracting a precious metal from the ore where premises, plant and machinery, labour and waste disposal costs are essential components of the refinement process, absorbing a large proportion of the precious metal's eventual sales value.

The overriding responsibility of a charity shop is to realise maximum residual value from the gift-in-kind donations it receives. An investment in shopfitting, stock generation and preparation etc. will enable a charity to realise maximum sales value from the donations it receives. The mantra "the better it's presented, the more it's worth" is particularly relevant to charity shop retailing. For this reason, an indifferent man's shirt dumped on a trestle table at a church hall jumble sale might fetch 25p, whereas that same shirt is likely to sell for £2.75 in a sweet-smelling, attractively lit, professionally managed and attractively merchandised charity shop. It follows that charities investing in shopfitting, display and training etc. will be able to enhance the perceived value of their stock and so make more sales and profit, thus justifying their investment. This benefit is reinforced by the strap-line on the Association of Charity Shops' Code of Charity Retailing logo: "Making the most of your donations".

Return on Capital Employed

Setting up shops will inevitably require initial capital funding which for a single shop might be as much as £50,000 although the average is likely to be nearer £15,000. **There is no point in a charity developing shops to raise funds unless it receives a return on its capital investment**, which is greater than might be expected from a safe interest bearing investment via a bank or blue chip shares etc. Though investment interest rates are currently low, it is still possible to receive 5% p.a. gross from some banks and building societies.

This means that for a shop where the capital investment has been £50,000, the shop must yield a minimum net profit of £2,500 p.a. and above to prove a better investment. Similarly, an initial investment of £20,000 must return a lesser £1,000.

Given that currently the average net profit per shop across the sector is nearly £17,000 p.a., most charity shops are returning a considerably greater return on their capital employed – assuming a typical investment of £15,000, this equates to a very satisfactory return on capital employed of 113% making charity shops, on average, a much higher yielding investment. However, there will inevitably be a handful of under-performing shops where the capital employed returns less and charities should be alert to this possibility. Similarly a charity's reserves of capital funding may be applied more productively in developing other forms of income generation such as an expansion of direct mailing appeals or legacy promotion.

Pareto's Principle – The 80-20 Rule

Charities running a large chain of shops will often find that a substantial proportion of their profits arise from a minority of their shops. This is a common outcome in business following the principle originally created by the Italian economist, Pareto, to describe the unequal distribution of wealth where 20% of the population owned 80% of the wealth. It has, however, a broader application whereby 20% of something is often responsible for 80% of the results.

Where this ratio does apply to a charity's shop chain, it is all too tempting to conclude that 80% of the shops should be closed keeping only the top performing 20% as this will result in more overall profit as a much smaller operation can be managed with considerably lower running costs.

Before reaching such a drastic conclusion, however, it should be recognised that the trading fortunes of individual shops can vary dramatically from one year to another resulting from changes in management, competition and the current viability of a particular location. Hence the top performing 20% of shops in one year may be a very different group in another year.

However, the rule should prompt a chain manager to concentrate their efforts on supporting and improving already successful shops rather than diverting every effort to improving under-performing shops. For example, 10% uplift in profits for a shop already netting £50,000 p.a. is equal to a 10% increase in profits for 10 shops producing profits of just £5,000 p.a. – what's more it takes considerably less effort, meaning that more high-performing shops can be tackled.

Additional Benefits

Besides raising funds in their own right, charity shops bring the following additional benefits:

- Their high street presence promotes the charity and its cause in the community. They are often the public face of the charity. This brings immeasurable but potentially substantial benefits – perhaps significant new income via legacy bequests and cash donations as well as attracting core volunteers.

- For national charities running hundreds of shops the promotional value of their shops fascias alone is worth a significant sum – perhaps millions of pounds when set against the cost of buying year round advertising through bill-boards and press/TV advertising. In particular, the recognition value of Oxfam's 748-shop presence on the high street must be enormous.

- They are 'green' in so far as they recycle clothing thus saving on the fuel and material production costs of new manufacture.

- They offer meaningful/worthwhile opportunities to volunteer and/or gain work experience.

- They benefit other traders in declining shopping communities by bringing trade and interest to the area.

- They offer a community service by providing a source of low-priced quality clothing to families in economic need.

- They are a source of consistent weekly income, which can often assist a charity with cash flow.

Major Concessions Received

Fortunately, because of their charitable status, charity shops are entitled to concessions that a commercial retailer does not enjoy. These are summarised below.

Relief from Uniform Business Rates

For charity shops selling 'wholly or mainly' donated goods, this relief is currently at the rate of 80% mandatory and 20% discretionary, meaning that all rating authorities must grant 80% relief and some may grant further discretionary relief up to a maximum of 20%. The mandatory relief is met by central government and is not a burden to local business ratepayers. These reliefs are a big concession for charity shops, reducing operating costs considerably.

Exemption from Profits Tax

Many overseas-based charities have considered adopting the UK model to raise funds through charity shops. However, for many it is not viable, as their governments would impose prohibitive tax on profits made through what is perceived as a straight trading activity. Happily, no such tax is levied in the UK on the sale of donated items. However, the significant and regular sale of purchased goods such as Christmas cards and gift lines must be operated through an independent trading company where any profits earned are paid back to the parent charity in a tax efficient way using Gift Aid thus avoiding tax.

Potential and Current Threats

As in any other commercial enterprise or fundraising activity, there will inevitably be current and potential threats to future success. The significant ones affecting charity shops are summarised as follows:

VAT on Sale of Donated Goods

The sale of donated goods in charity shops is currently zero-rated for VAT purposes, the most favourable VAT position. For many years there has been the threat that, under EU tax harmonisation, the standard rate of value added tax could be applied. This levy would have a dramatic effect on the sector eroding most of the profit currently generated. However, the Association of Charity Shops, together with other voluntary sector organisations, has forcefully argued the case on behalf of the sector for the retention of zero-rating and current indications are that there is no immediate threat.

Adjustment to Charity Relief on Uniform Business Rates

As mentioned above, charity shops are currently entitled to 80% mandatory relief and 20% discretionary relief from uniform business rates. These levels are extremely advantageous and have been in force for over 20 years, prior to which they were less generous at 50%.

For charities running large chains the value of these concessions runs into millions of pounds. Recent reviews of charitable rates relief have not resulted in any changes although there remains the possibility that present concessions may be changed. However, as with VAT harmonisation, the Association of Charity Shops has actively lobbied government on behalf of the sector stressing the negative impact that reduced concessions would have on the net funds available for charitable purposes.

Value Clothing Retailers

The advent of more and more value clothing retailers such as Peacocks, TK MAXX and Tesco has been a recent feature of the high street. National statistics show that, despite year on year overall inflation, in real terms the cost of clothing has actually reduced. For example, it is now possible to buy a brand new cotton/polyester shirt for £3.99 – this is a similar price to what many charity shops would charge for a pristine second hand one! Hence our sector has to combat new competition and will be forced to adjust its prices downwards to stay competitive. On the plus side, however, the availability of cheaper new clothing will mean that more will be purchased and therefore more available as potential donated stock, though it is likely to be of lower quality.

WEEE Directive

WEEE is an acronym for **Waste Electrical and Electronic Equipment** with such items being the fastest growing element in the municipal waste stream. Because there are so many hazardous substances used in electrical equipment (lead, cadmium, arsenic etc.) indiscriminate disposal poses a real threat of pollution to the environment. Accordingly, the directive places obligations on manufacturers and retailers of new electrical goods to take back electrical items from the public when new items are purchased and to recycle, reuse and dispose of these items responsibly. Although, for safety reasons, most charity shops do not generally sell mains electrical items, these will inevitably be donated and charity shops will have to bear the cost of disposal in compliance with the directive.

Sector Financial Performance

Comparative data for the sector's performance is published annually by *Charity Finance* magazine. Its publication is keenly awaited by charity shop chain managers eager to see how their charity has performed against all others and whether they have maintained or bettered their league position since the previous year.

The 2004/2005 survey included data from 97 charities representing 5,815 charity shops with the top 10 chains (ranked by total profit) accounting for 66% of total shop numbers and 70% of the total survey sample's profit.

Total income for 2004/2005 was recorded as £469m, which, after deducting operating expenses of £373.7m, left a profit of £95.3m - a margin of 20.3%. This means that, on average, **for every £1 spent in a charity shop, 79.7p is absorbed in running costs leaving 20.3p to support the charity**. Compared with more traditional forms of fundraising, this is a small return, but a high return compared with commercial retailing. However, as mentioned above, charity shops contribute additional income beyond their trading surpluses.

The performance of the smaller chains comprising **five shops or less** and representing 24 charities (25% of all charities reporting data) is better than the average for all shops. For these shops, the average margin of profit increases to 36.2% representing an average weekly profit per shop of £526 compared with £321 for all shops – 63.9% more.

Hospice shops perform particularly well with those running five shops or less (15 charities running 49 shops) returning a profit margin of 42.9% and an estimated average profit per shop per week of £600. For understandable reasons, hospices have a particularly emotive cause, which is more likely to touch the sympathies and support of the local community - this translates into higher levels of volunteer support and stock and cash donations.

Summary of 2004/2005 *Charity Finance* Survey

	Nos. Char-ities	Nos. Shops	Total Income £m	Total Profit £m	Profit Margin %	Av. Profit Per Shop Per Week £
All Shops	97	5,815	469.0	95.3	20.3	321
All Chains (1-5 shops)	24	75	5.8	2.1	36.2	526
Hospices (1-5 shops)	15	49	3.5	1.5	42.9	600

The statistics from the Charity Shops Survey are reproduced by kind permission of Charity Finance magazine. The 2004/2005 survey was published with the September 2005 issue of Charity Finance.

To help put the sector's overall profit margin into perspective, it is useful to compare it with the performance of some commercial chains. The latest results for four significant players are as follows:

Sample Profit Margins for Major Retailers

	Sales £m	Pre-tax profit £m	Profit margin %
Tesco	37,070	1,962	5.3
M&S	7,710	619	8.0
Primark	1,006	140	13.9
Peacocks	548	35	6.4

As can be seen, the sector's margin of 20.3% significantly outperforms these giants – and so it should!

2

Property Acquisitions

Although this section is primarily aimed at charities that are considering dipping their toe into setting up their first shop, it will also be relevant to those who already have one or two units established and need guidance before further development.

Basic Considerations

Running charity shops can be a risky business and there are easier and more productive ways for charities to raise funds. They are inherently expensive to run and demanding of resources. Their operation embraces a wide range of management responsibilities including: property management, shop fitting, managing paid staff and volunteers, stock generation and processing, pricing, promotion as well as, compliance with Health and Safety, Disability Discrimination, Employment and Consumer legislation etc.

Running medium-sized and even small chains can put great pressure on the often limited resources of a charity's HR, Finance and Secretary's/Legal departments. **Accordingly, when considering and costing a retail development programme, bear in mind the cost of these indirect, but nevertheless, essential support functions**.

Additionally, start up capital will be required for the first and subsequent shops. Typically, you will have to pay up-front for professional fees, shop-fitting, essential building repairs and the cost of recruiting and paying for staff in advance of the shop opening. Depending on the site and the standard required, such expenditure can typically range from £5 - £50,000.

Bear in mind that, based on the *Charity Finance* 2004-05 Charity Shops Survey, **the average charity shop in the UK produces a net surplus of just under £17,000 per year, which is equivalent to a margin of just 20.3% on sales.** Compared with more traditional forms of fundraising, this is a small return making charity shops, per se, one of the least productive forms of charity fundraising.

However, on a more upbeat note, it should be recognised that a charity shop's often prominent high street location brings additional benefits by promoting the charity and its cause in the community. In short, they are usually the public face of the charity. This can add substantial but immeasurable benefits – perhaps, significant new income via legacy bequests, cash donations as well as attracting core volunteers to your charity. These additional benefits are not always recognised by Trustees and seldom by Finance Directors!

Location

It is difficult to be too specific here as many shops both prosper and fail in a variety of similar locations. These can range from a sleepy market town with minimum pedestrian flow to hectic prime city centre high street sites. Arguably, the common ingredient for a successful charity shop is not its location alone but the fact that it has an effective and motivated manager. High calibre managers can equally be found in city centres or sleepy market towns.

A wise consultant, who recognised the great value of a good manager, was once asked to advise on ideal shop locations. He commented that the sector was doing things the wrong way round: "Surely better", he said, "to first find a good manager and then find a shop for him or her to run!" Although this comment was made slightly tongue in cheek, it holds more than an element of truth. After all, a charity shop manager has more influence on bottom line contribution than a commercial shop manager – she/he must be an effective pricer, merchandiser, stock generator, volunteer recruiter and local publicist – to say nothing of being scrupulously honest! So, whereas Tesco's mantra for business success is "location, location, location" ours might be "manager, manager, manager"!

Essentially, however, it is important that the chosen location offers a mixture of potential stock donors complemented by demand from people who want to purchase the donated stock. Bearing in mind that typical buyers are often on lower incomes and the people who donate stock are generally better off, an ideal location would be in an area that attracts both. For example, an area frequented by people from a nearby social housing estate coupled with people from an area of more affluent owner-occupied housing. However, in such a compact country as the UK, most shopping locations combine sufficient levels of both potential stock donors and buyers.

The ease with which stock donations can be made is another consideration. Locations having no parking restrictions have a big advantage as donors can drop off donations directly by car rather than lugging them from a remote car park. For this reason many would-be donors, though wanting to support a particular charity, may choose the one that is the most convenient. In a climate of ever increasing operating costs for the sector, there is a big advantage in avoiding or minimising the need to run a costly house-to-house bag drop collection operation.

One common sense and effective way to asses the likely success of a potential unit is to seek the opinion of neighbouring shopkeepers – there are none more qualified to offer local advice and usually they are all too willing and flattered to share it. Snippets of information such as a planned change of bus route, the imminent closure of the Post Office or the intended imposition of double yellow lines can be invaluable intelligence.

Size

The sales area of a typical charity shop ranges from as little as 200 square feet to well over 1000. However, most are around 500-600 square feet, which is roughly equivalent to between 50 and 60 square metres. Bearing in mind that the range and variety of stock they have to carry, 500-600 square feet is normally sufficient. If the intention is to include a furniture section or a stand-alone furniture shop then more square footage will be necessary.

Passers-by (Pedestrian Flow)

The people who pass a shop are all potential buyers and/or stock providers. Therefore, it is important to access numbers when evaluating a new site. This is normally measured in passers-by per hour (or footfall). There are no hard and fast rules about essential minimums. Some charity shops boast phenomenal sales and profits from pedestrian flows of as little as 100 per hour. **However, in most cases, a minimum flow of 300 per hour is desirable.** This can be measured by counting the people who pass by for 10-minute periods over, say, three different trading times, then taking the average and multiplying the result by six to give the hourly average. Hence, an average of 50 in 10 minutes equates to the desired 300 per hour.

Research by one charity running a large chain of shops showed that high pedestrian flow did not always translate into high sales. It found that in its less busy village/market town/small community type locations the conversion rate from passer-by to customer was much higher than with their busy prime site, locations. This proved to be a useful and significant finding, especially as busy prime sites suffer higher rents and business rates! Furthermore, non-town/city centre sites generally attract more volunteers and through-the-door stock donations; all of which helps to keep operating costs down and profits up.

Building Configuration and Compliances

In addition to the requirement for between 500 and 600 square feet of retail selling space, you should add a minimum of 300 square feet for storage and preparation. In the interests of operating efficiency and convenience for the (often elderly) volunteers, it is desirable to have this facility on the ground floor immediately behind the sales area. However, with many locations, the only available area is on an upper floor or in a basement. Provided that the retail footage and pedestrian flow minimum requirements are met, you may have to accept a less than ideal storage/preparation facility.

Your selected unit will also have to comply with both Health & Safety and the more recently introduced Disability Discrimination

Act. Such compliance can be a costly business especially if the previous tenant or landlord had neglected their responsibilities. Charities, by their very nature, are perceived as responsible and caring organisations. Hence, there may be a greater expectation of compliance from staff, volunteers and the general public than might be expected at the corner newsagent.

Comprehensive guidance on this legislation is provided by the Association of Charity Shops in its Members' Handbook.

Proximity to Other Charity Shops

A frequent question for those considering a good location is whether it is beneficial or not to open a shop near to or remote from other charity shops. Opinions on this differ with some arguing that it is an advantage to be in close proximity to other similar shops; especially as in the commercial world, similar business sometimes flock together to attract like-minded customers seeking a specific good or service. An example being the concentration of shops in London's Tottenham Court Road, selling electronic goods. Likewise, many towns and cities have an area devoted to wine bars and restaurants.

Others hold the view that it is better for a charity shop to be located away from competitors as all are competing for the same stock and custom. In other words, the more the offer is diluted the less support each shop will attract.

As with so many aspects of charity shop retailing, there is no hard and fast rule, though experience does show that, on balance, it is beneficial to be in close proximity to some but not too many competitors after which, based on one charity's research, there is a diminishing return. As a rule of thumb, to have more than say, half a dozen competitors within a half-mile radius should give cause for concern.

Local Considerations

Whilst the above guidance would apply to any charity, there may be considerations that are specific to a particular charity. For instance, a locally supported charity such as a hospice or church may be restricted to establishing a shop/s within the confines of its operating area. Conversely, a charity with a larger geographical spread or even national coverage may want to locate a new shop in an area where it is not currently represented with a view to gaining additional profile as well as raising funds. In the latter eventuality, presence may take some preference over profit.

Whether your charity is locally or nationally based, your preferred location might be influenced by whether or not, in a particular area, you already have a pool of potential shop volunteers. Charities that operate group/branch services at a local level often have would-be shop volunteers waiting in the wings. With volunteers being such an essential and valuable resource, this gives a big advantage.

Terms of Occupation

Depending on the resources available coupled with the level of risk you want to take, there are a number of options covering the terms for occupying a retail premises.

Minimum Risk

Charities can go down the "suck it and see" route whereby they take temporary occupancy on a shop that is on the market for sale or letting. Alternatively, it may be a shop that is imminently due for demolition as part of a local authority development programme. These shops can be found by approaching the estates departments of local authorities and large corporations, which run or manage retail premises.

Such shops are normally acquired on a simple licence agreement whereby the charity undertakes to pay all the associated running costs and gives an undertaking to vacate at very short notice, usually twenty-four hours. These units are available on a rent-free or nominal rent basis. In cases where the shop is on the market for letting, a particular advantage of this type of occupancy is that the charity has an opportunity to assess whether or not it is worthwhile taking a permanent lease. In effect, the charity will have had a probationary period when known past sales will determine whether the shop can still operate effectively bearing the added expense of the market rental.

Higher Risk

From the outset, charities may prefer to seek leasehold premises where a fixed term of occupancy is guaranteed, albeit with all the associated and the often onerous liabilities of a formal lease. If this is the preferred approach, the charity should seek out an estate agent who specialises in the commercial property market. They should be briefed on your preferred location, square footage/metre and maximum rental requirements. Once a site is found that meets these requirements, you will need to instruct a property surveyor to survey the property, negotiate on your behalf and find a solicitor to handle the conveyancing.

It is worth mentioning that charities are generally regarded as "good covenants" – in other words, they are likely to honour their lease covenants compared with, for instance, a sole trader who may have no track record and wants to invest redundancy money in a somewhat speculative and unproven retail enterprise.

You should instruct your agent to use this good covenant to advantage by negotiating, the most favourable lease terms for a new lease by way of rental level, repairing obligations and break clause. **A break clause allows you to terminate the lease after, say two years, despite the fact that the lease runs for a longer period. These break clauses are a useful escape route if trading falls below expectations and you want to terminate your lease before the formal expiry of the lease.**

Freehold Acquisitions

As part of their property portfolios, some charities own shops outright, which were originally purchased on a freehold basis. Due to the recent buoyant commercial property market, these acquisitions have proved a sound investment as the resale value is invariably far in excess of the original purchase price. As such, they are potentially a useful means of raising cash by selling on. Where a freehold shop is trading successfully and the charity wants to continue in occupation, it can consider a sale and leaseback arrangement where the freehold is sold to a third party on the understanding that the charity remains in occupation as a tenant of the new owner under a formal lease.

In reality however, not many charities are in the enviable position of having sufficient reserves to purchase shop freeholds; even if they did, there remains the question of whether it would be acceptable for a charity to use its funds in this way as opposed to deploying them on front line services in direct support of its charitable objectives. Where freehold shops are held, however, so as not to distort performance, it is important to apply a market rent before arriving at net contribution. After all, the parent charity would receive a market rent were the premises let to a third party tenant.

The acquisition of property is a complex subject and expert advice should always be taken. Additional information and guidance is provided in the Association of Charity Shops' Members' Handbook.

Site Evaluation and Financial Forecasts

Site Evaluation Questionnaire

It is a good practice, when arriving at a decision on one or a number of prospective new sites, to adopt a systemised approach where the features of each can be compared and a formal record made of whether the unit/s meet the minimum criteria. **The New Site Evaluation questionnaire, Appendix A** is provided for this purpose and covers many of the aspects already referred to above.

Although fairly comprehensive, you may want to modify this form to include questions specific to your needs. Linked with the questionnaire should be your budget or income and expenditure forecast. **Example Spreadsheets (A-E) are provided with Appendix B.** Depending on your charity's sign-off procedures, you may care to use the combined documents (Appendices A&B) as your business case seeking formal approval from your manager/Trustees to proceed to acquisition.

Financial Forecasts/Budgets

For any new enterprise, be it a charity mailing appeal, a fundraising event or a charity shop, it is always difficult to predict with any degree of accuracy what your final income and

27

expenditure will be. Even the big name supermarkets sometimes get it wildly wrong when forecasting sales for a refurbished or new store.

Obviously, it helps if your proposed new shop is an addition to an already established chain, as you may have comparable performance data for similar sites. However, where this is a first unit or an addition to just a handful of established shops, it is more difficult. It is always better to err on the side of caution adopting a somewhat pessimistic approach – Finance Directors and their ilk are always impressed when an activity comes in at on or above budget whereas a shortfall, albeit that a significant surplus has been made, is regarded as failure.

Too many managers budget for what they want to happen rather than what is likely to happen. For instance, when preparing a budget for an existing shop, which they know is under-performing, they often make optimistic assumptions about everything coming right next year: "We will start that new shop fit in April, turn that negative attitude of the shop manager around and open on Sundays during the summer months – all this will give us another ten thousand on the bottom line." In reality however, the funds for the shop fit were not forthcoming until December, the manager remained intransigent and the local committee was dead against Sunday trading!

Accepting that the overriding purpose of a charity shop is to raise net funds, it is important to set a minimum acceptable level of net contribution and profit margin. The example income and expenditure statements (Appendix B) assume these minimums to be **£10,000 of net profit in a full year's trading AND a profit margin of no less than 25% on sales.**

It is recommended that, for any prospective new shop, both minimums be met. For instance, a profit of £12,000 at a margin of 15% would not be acceptable; nor would a margin of 30% on a profit of £9,000. By setting a margin minimum, you have a better chance of protecting profit should income fall – **a shop producing a credible profit of £20,000 on a precarious margin of just 10% could LOSE that same amount should sales fall by 20%.**

Some established charity chains set these minimums higher, but those recommended are, we believe, a sensible starting point and you may, of course, change them to a level acceptable to your organisation.

The sample Income and Expenditure forms, (Appendix B) have been set up as a Microsoft Excel spreadsheet *(available electronically from the Association of Charity Shops when the book is purchased)* on which you simply input your estimated values in the fourth column and the calculations are made automatically.

Apart from giving a full year's figures, you will note that the form also allows you to estimate for part of a year as completion of a new lease seldom occurs on the very first day of a new financial year! To calculate part-year estimates, simply input as indicated the number of weeks you anticipate the shop will trade during the remainder of the year. **Please note that the formulae assume that you will incur four weeks of expenditure for most expenditure items before you open for trading**. This is because a paid manager will invariably be in place helping to set up the shop. Furthermore, you will be responsible for all associated property costs from the date of Completion, which is assumed to be four weeks before opening.

Please note also:

- Against row F, the spreadsheet calculates the weekly sales required to break-even and against row G, the weekly sales required to net the recommended minimum profit of £10,000 p.a.

- It is assumed that any capital expenditure will be depreciated over five years

- No account is taken of indirect expenses i.e. the cost, where applicable, of an area manager plus all the associated charity support costs.

Specific comments against the Examples (Appendix B):

Example A

Based on the estimates, this is a viable unit as it exceeds the minimums at both profit and margin levels - £21,500 and 26.9% respectfully.

Example B
Danger signals here, as although the profit is just about acceptable, the margin at 19% is not. Reject.

Example C
Providing the sales estimates are roughly right, this is potentially a very profitable shop, despite the relatively high salary and rental costs. Bear in mind however, that the unit has to take a significant £1,660 per week just to break-even.

Example D
This is a blank form **with the formulas included**. On request, the Association of Charity Shops will e-mail you a copy for you to input your estimates.

Example E
Another blank form, but this time **without formulas**. On this blank page you can fill in your estimates manually.

ANY CHARITY
NEW SHOP SITE EVALUATION | Appendix A |

LOCATION AND GENERAL INFORMATION

Site Address:

Post code

Total Square Footage: _____ sq. ft.

Situation:
(please circle)

Town Centre   Main Shopping Area
Secondary Shopping Area   Edge of Town
Other *(please specify)* _____

Adjacent properties (name & business):
_____
_____
_____

LOCAL INFORMATION   N.B. The majority of this information can be obtained from the estate agents and/or their property particulars

Town Pop. [   ]   Market Day [   ]   Half Day Closing [   ]

Retail Catchment Population [   ]   No. of Council Estates [   ]   Late Night Shopping Day [   ]

Which major chain stores are in the town? *(please list)*
_____
_____
_____

What are the comments from local traders about trading patterns, market conditions and location suitability etc.:
_____
_____
_____
_____
_____

31

PEDESTRIAN FLOW

Usually a successful charity shop requires a minimum average of 300 passers-by per hour. Count the passers-by at three different times (e.g. busy, quiet, in between) for 10 minutes, take the average, and multiply by six to give the total per hour. Then take an average of the three results. *Include only potential customers i.e. people you estimate to be over 12 years of age and who pass within, say, 10 feet of the shop front.*

#	Date	Start time	Stop time	Number	Passers-by per hour
1					
2					
3					

Average per hour

Weather Conditions   1._____
2._____
3._____

Are the majority *(please circle):*   Window Shopping

Not Looking   Other

Are these counts likely to be typical?   Y   N

Comment:

_____
_____
_____
_____
_____
_____
_____
_____
_____

COMPETITION

How far is it to: The nearest *Any Charity* Shop?

_____

The nearest *Any Charity* Branch/Centre

_____

Do you anticipate local support from an *Any Charity*   Y   N
local Branch/Centre in providing volunteers etc.?

Comment:
_____
_____
_____
_____
_____

Please list all other charity shops in the shopping locality

Charity	Approx Distance Away *(mtrs)*	Charity	Approx Distance Away *(mtrs)*
1.		8.	
2.		9.	
3.		10.	
4.		11.	
5.		12.	
6.		13.	
7.		14.	

Are you aware of any charity house-to-house   Y   N
clothing/bric-a-brac collections in the area?

DETAILED PREMISES INFORMATION

GENERAL

Is the lease an   Assignment   Underlease   New Lease

(please circle):   Internal repairing only   Full repairing/insuring

Length of lease: _____ years

How often are Rent Reviews? _____ years

Is there a Break Clause?   Y   N

When do you estimate the premises were built? _____

Annual Rent	£	**Annual Service Charge (if any)**	£
Initial premium (if any)	£	***Annual Business Rate**	£

* Amount payable before charitable relief. This can be obtained by telephoning the Local Rating Authority.

How many floors does the accommodation consist of? _____ floors

Where is the Storage /Preparation area sited? *(please circle)*   Basement / Ground / Upper

Sq. Footage Breakdown:

Sales Floor		Storage/ Preparation		Other	

Is there a residential tenant in situ?   Y   N

If Yes, how much is the rent receivable p.a.   £_____

When is the site available for possession? _____

What is the current or last business? _____

Does the shop have a flush fronted/recess door   Y   N

Does the building contain any accommodation not included in this lease?   Y   N

If yes, what does this include? _____

Does this additional accommodation have separate access?   Y   N

DETAILED PREMISES INFORMATION
(Continued)

EXTERIOR

How many (if any) parking spaces are offered?

Is the access for loading/unloading at: Front   Rear of shop
(please circle)

Are there parking restrictions outside of shop?   Y   N

If Yes, what are they?   Single yellow lines   Meter
(please circle)   Double yellow lines   Time limited

Is any land included with the premises?   Y   N

How much/What?

How far is it to the nearest: Bank   _____metres
      Bus Stop   _____metres
      Car Park   _____metres
      Post Office   _____metres
      Pedestrian Crossing   _____metres

Does the exterior appear to be in good repair?   Y   N

Is there a security system in place?   Y   N

Please detail any exterior repairs which you estimate will be required before opening:

_____
_____
_____
_____
_____
_____
_____
_____
_____
_____
_____

DETAILED PREMISES INFORMATION
(Continued)   INTERIOR

How is the shop heated?

_____

Is this adequate for our needs?   Y   N

Is there a: Telephone line   Y   N
                   W.C.   Y   N
                   Hot Water   Y   N

Are any fixtures and fittings included?   Y   N

What? _____

How would you describe the state of repair of the interior?
Very Good   Good   Adequate   Poor

Please detail any interior repairs which you estimate to be required before opening:
_____
_____
_____

HEALTH AND SAFETY

Are the corridors and stairways adequately lit?   Y   N

Do the stair handrails appear to be secure and at the right height?   Y   N   N/A

Are there any trapdoors leading to a basement area?   Y   N

Is there a smoke alarm?   Y   N

Does the designated stock room/preparation area have natural light?   Y   N

Does the designated stock room/preparation area have ventilation (window opening or Xpelair extractor fan)?   Y   N

Would staff vacating the premises from a rear/side exit be exposed to an unlit/isolated area where they may be vulnerable to attack?   Y   N

Has an asbestos survey been completed and, where applicable, action taken to deal with any asbestos found?   Y   N   N/A

DISABILITY DISCRIMINATION
Do the premises comply with the basic requirements of the Act:

MAIN ENTRANCE

Are all main entrances level with the pavement?	Y	N	
If not, is there room for a ramp?	Y	N	N/A
Does the entrance door have a clear opening of at least 800mm / 2.63ft?	Y	N	

GENERAL

Is/Are there foot-wipe mat(s)?	Y	N	
If so, are they level (i.e. recessed) with the floor surface?	Y	N	N/A
Can a wheelchair user turn (1.5m required) and move around the ground floor of the premises?	Y	N	
Are there corridors?	Y	N	
If so, are they wide enough (0.9m, and 1.5m to turn) for a wheelchair user?	Y	N	N/A

STAIRWAYS

Do you plan essential activities upstairs or downstairs (i.e. sales floor, stock room, preparation area etc)?	Y	N	
If yes, do the stairways have a handrail?	Y	N	N/A
Are the step nosings (rounded edge of steps) in a contrasting colour?	Y	N	N/A
Are step treads made of a non-slip material?	Y	N	N/A

TOILET(S)

Is there a toilet (2m x 1.5m) which can be entered by a wheelchair-user?	Y	N	
Is there a toilet cubicle specifically designed for use by disabled people?	Y	N	

FIRE EXITS

Are there Fire Exit doors with panic bars?	Y	N	
If so, are they of sufficient width (800mm) to accommodate a wheelchair?	Y	N	N/A
Is the immediate exterior surface area suitable for wheelchair use?	Y	N	

OTHER GENERAL COMMENTS ABOUT THE PREMISES

_____
_____
_____
_____
_____
_____
_____
_____
_____
_____
_____

Signed *Any Charity* Retail Manager   ....

Date   ....

APPROVAL

I recommend/do not recommend that these premises be acquired.
Where recommended, I confirm that:

a)   the shop satisfies *Any Charity's* requirements in terms of location, volunteer availability and management resource etc.

b)   the shop is within the current year's Operating Plan and Budget and that the net income forecast, as detailed on the attached *Estimated Income and Expenditure sheet,* is not less than budget.

Where not recommended please state reasons:

_____
_____
_____
_____
_____
_____
_____

Signed *Any Charity* Senior Manager ....

Date   ....

Any Charity **APPENDIX B** Example **A**
ESTIMATED INCOME & EXPENDITURE FOR PROPOSED NEW SHOP
At: 79 High Street Anytown

Input anticipated full weeks trading in current financial year | **26** | Wks

		Remainder of current year (viii)	Av. per Week £	Complete this column first — Per Full Year £	As % of Sales
	INCOME				
A	Sales	40,000	1,538	80,000	100.0%
B	**LESS** Bag Drop Costs	2,885	96	5,000	6.3%
C	**GROSS PROFIT (A-B)**	37,115	1,442	75,000	93.8%
	EXPENSES				
	Salaries including NI	9,808	326.92	17,000	21.3%
	Recruitment	500	9.62	500	0.6%
	Volunteer Expenses	1,154	38.46	2,000	2.5%
	Advertising	2,885	96.15	5,000	6.3%
	*Rent payable	8,654	288.46	15,000	18.8%
	*Service Charge	1,154	38.46	2,000	2.5%
	*Rates - General (i)	692	23.08	1,200	1.5%
	Rates - Water	288	9.62	500	0.6%
	Premises Maintenance including equipment	577	19.23	1,000	1.3%
	Electricity	577	19.23	1,000	1.3%
	Gas	-	-		0.0%
	Insurance (ii)	173	5.77	300	0.4%
	Telephone	577	19.23	1,000	1.3%
	Postage	115	3.85	200	0.3%
	Professional Fees (iii)	3,000	57.69	3,000	3.8%
	Depreciation (iv)	2,192	73.08	3,800	4.8%
	Other		-		0.0%
D	**TOTAL EXPENSES**	32,346	1,028.85	53,500	66.9%
E	**PROFIT (C - D) (Vii)**	4,769	413.46	21,500	26.9%
F	*Weekly sales required to break-even (v)*			1,125	
G	*Weekly sales required to net £10,000 pa*			1,317	
H	**CAPITAL EXPENSES**				
	Repairs & Renewals - Shopfit & Equipment (vi)			12,000	
	Repairs & Renewals - Essential Building Repairs			5,000	
	Estimated DDA compliance costs			2,000	
I	**TOTAL CAPITAL EXPENSES**			19,000	

Signed .... Dated ....

NOTES:
(i)   Assume 80% mandatory relief only
(ii)   Include 3rd party Public Liability & where applicable re-embursement of landlord's building insurance
          & separate cover for plate glass windows
(iii)   To include solicitors & surveyors fees etc on acquisition
(iv)   Capital costs (per Capital Expenses box) amortised over 5 years or expiry of the lease which ever is the lesser
(v)   Total Expenses (D) + Bag Drop Costs (B) divided by 52 weeks
(vi)   To include till & display equipment etc.
(vii)   **Should not be less than £10,000 AND no less than 25% of total sales**
(viii)   *Remainder of Current Year* values assume that the majority of expenses will be incurred proportionally
          4 weeks before opening day on Completion
*   Available from Estate Agents particulars

Any Charity   APPENDIX B   Example B
ESTIMATED INCOME & EXPENDITURE FOR PROPOSED NEW SHOP
At: 116 The Broadway Anywhere

Input anticipated full weeks trading in current financial year | **13** | Wks

		Remainder of current year (viii)	Av. per Week £	Complete this column first Per Full Year £	As % of Sales
	INCOME				
A	Sales	13,750	1,058	55,000	100.0%
B	**LESS** Bag Drop Costs	490	29	1,500	2.7%
C	**GROSS PROFIT (A-B)**	13,260	1,029	53,500	97.3%
	EXPENSES				
	Salaries including NI	4,904	288.46	15,000	27.3%
	Recruitment	500	9.62	500	0.9%
	Volunteer Expenses	490	28.85	1,500	2.7%
	Advertising	981	57.69	3,000	5.5%
	*Rent payable	3,923	230.77	12,000	21.8%
	*Service Charge	-	-		0.0%
	*Rates - General (i)	262	15.38	800	1.5%
	Rates - Water	114	6.73	350	0.6%
	Premises Maintenance including equipment	327	19.23	1,000	1.8%
	Electricity	327	19.23	1,000	1.8%
	Gas	-	-		0.0%
	Insurance (ii)	98	5.77	300	0.5%
	Telephone	327	19.23	1,000	1.8%
	Postage	65	3.85	200	0.4%
	Professional Fees (iii)	3,000	57.69	3,000	5.5%
	Depreciation (iv)	1,112	65.38	3,400	6.2%
	Other		-		0.0%
D	**TOTAL EXPENSES**	16,430	827.88	43,050	78.3%
E	**PROFIT (C - D) (Vii)**	- 3,170	200.96	10,450	19.0%
F	*Weekly sales required to break-even (v)*			857	
G	*Weekly sales required to net £10,000 pa*			1,049	
H	**CAPITAL EXPENSES**				
	Repairs & Renewals - Shopfit & Equipment (vi)			10,000	
	Repairs & Renewals - Essential Building Repairs			5,000	
	Estimated DDA compliance costs			2,000	
I	**TOTAL CAPITAL EXPENSES**			**17,000**	

Signed ....   Dated ....

NOTES:
(i)	Assume 80% mandatory relief only
(ii)	Include 3rd party Public Liability & where applicable re-embursement of landlord's building insurance & separate cover for plate glass windows
(iii)	To include solicitors & surveyors fees etc on acquisition
(iv)	Capital costs (per Capital Expenses box) amortised over 5 years or expiry of the lease which ever is the lesser
(v)	Total Expenses (D) + Bag Drop Costs Costs (B) divided by 52 weeks
(vi)	To include till & display equipment etc.
(vii)	**Should not be less than £10,000 AND no less than 25% of total sales**
(viii)	*Remainder of Current Year* values assume that the majority of expenses will be incurred proportionally 4 weeks before opening day on Completion
*	Available from Estate Agents particulars

Any Charity APPENDIX B Example C
ESTIMATED INCOME & EXPENDITURE FOR PROPOSED NEW SHOP
At: 278 Main Street Anycity

Input anticipated full weeks trading in current financial year | **39** | Wks

		Remainder of current year (viii)	Av. per Week £	Complete this column first Per Full Year £	As % of Sales
	INCOME				
A	Sales	93,750	2,404	125,000	100.0%
B	**LESS** Bag Drop Costs	5,788	135	7,000	5.6%
C	**GROSS PROFIT (A-B)**	87,962	2,269	118,000	94.4%
	EXPENSES				
	Salaries including NI	20,673	480.77	25,000	20.0%
	Recruitment	1,000	19.23	1,000	0.8%
	Volunteer Expenses	1,654	38.46	2,000	1.6%
	Advertising	4,135	96.15	5,000	4.0%
	*Rent payable	20,673	480.77	25,000	20.0%
	*Service Charge	1,654	38.46	2,000	1.6%
	*Rates - General (i)	3,308	76.92	4,000	3.2%
	Rates - Water	1,240	28.85	1,500	1.2%
	Premises Maintenance including equipment	827	19.23	1,000	0.8%
	Electricity	1,240	28.85	1,500	1.2%
	Gas	-	-		0.0%
	Insurance (ii)	248	5.77	300	0.2%
	Telephone	1,240	28.85	1,500	1.2%
	Postage	165	3.85	200	0.2%
	Professional Fees (iii)	3,000	57.69	3,000	2.4%
	Depreciation (iv)	5,210	121.15	6,300	5.0%
	Other		-		0.0%
D	**TOTAL EXPENSES**	66,267	1,525.00	79,300	63.4%
E	PROFIT (C - D) (Vii)	21,694	744.23	38,700	31.0%
F	*Weekly sales required to break-even (v)*			1,660	
G	*Weekly sales required to net £10,000 pa*			1,852	
H	**CAPITAL EXPENSES**				
	Repairs & Renewals - Shopfit & Equipment (vi)			20,000	
	Repairs & Renewals - Essential Building Repairs			7,500	
	Estimated DDA compliance costs			4,000	
I	**TOTAL CAPITAL EXPENSES**			31,500	

Signed .... Dated ....

NOTES:
(i) Assume 80% mandatory relief only
(ii) Include 3rd party Public Liability & where applicable re-embursement of landlord's building insurance & separate cover for plate glass windows
(iii) To include solicitors & surveyors fees etc on acquisition
(iv) Capital costs (per Capital Expenses box) amortised over 5 years or expiry of the lease which ever is the lesser
(v) Total Expenses (D) + Bag Drop Costs Costs (B) divided by 52 weeks
(vi) To include till & display equipment etc.
(vii) **Should not be less than £10,000 AND no less than 25% of total sales**
(viii) *Remainder of Current Year* values assume that the majority of expenses will be incurred proportionally 4 weeks before opening day on Completion
* Available from Estate Agents particulars

Any Charity APPENDIX B Example D
ESTIMATED INCOME & EXPENDITURE FOR PROPOSED NEW SHOP

At --

Input anticipated full weeks trading in current financial year [   ] **Wks**

(electronic version with formulae available from the Association of Charity shops)

	Remainder of current year (viii)	Av. per Week £	Complete this column first — Per Full Year £	As % of Sales
INCOME				
A Sales	-			#DIV/0!
B LESS Bag Drop Costs	-	-		#DIV/0!
C GROSS PROFIT (A-B)	-	-	-	#DIV/0!
EXPENSES				
Salaries including NI	-	-		#DIV/0!
Recruitment	-	-		#DIV/0!
Volunteer Expenses	-	-		#DIV/0!
Advertising	-	-		#DIV/0!
*Rent payable	-	-		#DIV/0!
*Service Charge	-	-		#DIV/0!
*Rates - General (i)	-	-		#DIV/0!
Rates - Water	-	-		#DIV/0!
Premises Maintenance including equipment	-	-		#DIV/0!
Electricity	-	-		#DIV/0!
Gas	-	-		#DIV/0!
Insurance (ii)	-	-		#DIV/0!
Telephone	-	-		#DIV/0!
Postage	-	-		#DIV/0!
Professional Fees (iii)	-	-		#DIV/0!
Depreciation (iv)	-	-		#DIV/0!
Other		-		#DIV/0!
D TOTAL EXPENSES	-	-		#DIV/0!
E PROFIT (C - D) (Vii)	-	-		#DIV/0!
F *Weekly sales required to break-even (v)*			-	
G *Weekly sales required to net £10,000 pa*				
H **CAPITAL EXPENSES**				
Repairs & Renewals - Shopfit & Equipment (vi)				
Repairs & Renewals - Essential Building Repairs				
Estimated DDA compliance costs				
I TOTAL CAPITAL EXPENSES			-	

Signed .... Dated ....

NOTES:
(i) Assume 80% mandatory relief only
(ii) Include 3rd party Public Liability & where applicable re-embursement of landlord's building insurance & separate cover for plate glass windows
(iii) To include solicitors & surveyors fees etc on acquisition
(iv) Capital costs (per Capital Expenses box) amortised over 5 years or expiry of the lease which ever is the lesser
(v) Total Expenses (D) + Bag Drop Costs Costs (B) divided by 52 weeks
(vi) To include till & display equipment etc.
(vii) **Should not be less than £10,000 AND no less than 25% of total sales**
(viii) *Remainder of Current Year* values assume that the majority of expenses will be incurred proportionally 4 weeks before opening day on Completion
* Available from Estate Agents particulars

Any Charity **APPENDIX B Example E**

ESTIMATED INCOME & EXPENDITURE FOR PROPOSED NEW SHOP

At --

Input anticipated full weeks trading in current financial year		**Wks**

(Blank for manual completion)

		Remainder of current year (viii)	Av. per Week £	*Complete this column first* Per Full Year £	As % of Sales
	INCOME				
A	Sales				
B	**LESS** Bag Drop Costs				
C	**GROSS PROFIT (A-B)**				
	EXPENSES				
	Salaries including NI				
	Recruitment				
	Volunteer Expenses				
	Advertising				
	*Rent payable				
	*Service Charge				
	*Rates - General (i)				
	Rates - Water				
	Premises Maintenance including equipment				
	Electricity				
	Gas				
	Insurance (ii)				
	Telephone				
	Postage				
	Professional Fees (iii)				
	Depreciation (iv)				
	Other				
D	**TOTAL EXPENSES**				
E	**PROFIT (C - D) (Vii)**				
F	*Weekly sales required to break-even (v)*				
G	*Weekly sales required to net £10,000 pa*				
H	**CAPITAL EXPENSES**				
	Repairs & Renewals - Shopfit & Equipment (vi)				
	Repairs & Renewals - Essential Building Repairs				
	Estimated DDA compliance costs				
I	**TOTAL CAPITAL EXPENSES**				

Signed …………………………….   Dated ………………………..

NOTES:
(i)   Assume 80% mandatory relief only
(ii) Include 3rd party Public Liability & where applicable re-embursement of landlord's building insurance
      & separate cover for plate glass windows
(iii) To include solicitors & surveyors fees etc on acquisition
(iv) Capital costs (per Capital Expenses box) amortised over 5 years or expiry of the lease which ever is the lesser
(v)   Total Expenses (D) + Bag Drop Costs Costs (B) divided by 52 weeks
(vi) To include till & display equipment etc.
(vii) **Should not be less than £10,000 AND no less than 25% of total sales**
(viii) *Remainder of Current Year* values assume that the majority of expenses will be incurred proportionally
       4 weeks before opening day on Completion
*   Available from Estate Agents particulars

3

Shopfitting, Display & Layout

Unique Considerations

A typical charity shop will generate approximately 70% of its sales from clothing and 30% from items generically referred to as bric-a-brac comprising books, ornaments, toys, costume jewellery and household textiles etc. This stock composition is not pre-planned (as would be the case with a commercial retailer) but is simply a reflection of the type and quantities of donations that charity shops receive. Accordingly, the shopfit and layout chosen must be appropriate for our particular "stock in trade" and will comprise mainly of rails for the clothing and shelving for the bric-a-brac.

An important difference between our shops and commercial clothing shops is that every item we display for sale is a unique piece of merchandise – unlike, for instance, M&S who would carry back-up stocks of a particular clothing item in all sizes and colours.

Unless we display as much stock as possible, the chances of matching an item to the needs of a customer will be reduced and sales lost.

An analogy is the second-hand car business - a dealer having a forecourt that can accommodate only 10 used cars will not sell as many as one who can display 50 cars. Similar models and makes of car will come in different colours and levels of wear and tear etc. Hence, the more that is on view, the greater the chance of matching the customer's requirement.

The antithesis would be the high-end retailers such as Bond Street jewellers or Knightsbridge designer shops where 'less' gives more impact than 'more', but charity shops are at the other end of the spectrum – we sell on variety and price, the others sell on exclusivity.

Stock Density

Though accepting the principle that "if it's not on display it won't sell", care must be taken to ensure that clothing items are not unduly crammed on the rails. It should be possible for customers to easily remove or separate an item on the rail to inspect its features - as such there must be sufficient slack. As a rule of thumb, the right density has been reached when, fully compressed, the items occupy two-thirds of the rail leaving one third free.

The majority of women's and men's clothing is half-length to be worn either above or below the waist. Charity shops often wrongly display these half-length items on a full-length rail instead of a two-tier one. This under utilises the available display space and hinders the achievement of optimum stock density. The importance of this was realised as early as the 1970s when charities began to open permanent units and invest in custom shopfits. Two-tier rails replaced the old single freestanding ones, dramatically increasing items on display and resulting in much higher sales.

When assessing the overall stock density of hanging items, the following simple ratio is a useful yardstick – **minimum of two hanging items per square foot of display space.** This means, for example, that a shop with a sales area of 500 square feet devoted to hanging items should have a minimum of 1,000 items on display. A lower ratio means that the shop is operating inefficiently and will lose sales, as a proportion of its unique stock will not be displayed.

Too many charity shops are guilty of under-display due to a poor shopfit or an inefficient stock replenishment system or both. Accepting the correlation between items on display and sales, we can estimate that **a shortfall on optimum items displayed of just 10% could result in a weekly loss of sales of £200** for a typical shop – that's £10,000 per annum and that's probably all lost profit!

A final reminder – **if an item can be hung, it should be hung.** It's much tidier that way and easier for the customer to inspect. Attempts by charity shops to ape their commercial counterparts by building neat piles of folded jumpers, trousers and shirts are definitely not recommended – they are wrecked in minutes by eager customers and require constant maintenance.

Proportionate Display

This is a pompous description of a very simple concept. It is a technique used by many department stores. Essentially it means that the amount of footage occupied by a department or range of goods should be in proportion to its sales. It is applied rigorously in food supermarkets where every square foot must "pay its way" or as one food retailer so graphically described, "sweat"!

As most of the sales in charity shops arise from women's clothing (usually 50%), then theoretically 50% of the shop's display space should be allocated to this department. Similarly, if books account for 10% they warrant 10% of the shop's display space.

Although the technique has a useful application for our sector, it need not be applied too rigidly. However, it may help to highlight a serious case of 'over-display' where, for example, an entire wall is given over to a sparsely populated display of low-value bric-a-brac contributing a meagre £50 per week but occupying 25% of the footage available. For a shop taking £1,000 per week, such performance deserves only 5% and unless reduced will deprive more lucrative departments of additional display space and all-important additional sales.

Positioning

Demand Product

There are no hard and fast rules concerning the positioning of the various departments within the shop. Basically, there are two schools of thought and, like so many aspects of retailing, they can be tested to see which one is the more effective.

The first is the deliberate promotion of the best selling or 'demand' product by giving it the most prominent position within the shop –

in our case women's clothing. Hence, womenswear would be featured at the front of the shop with less-in-demand products such as menswear and household textiles etc. relegated to the rear or a basement/first floor.

The promotion of best sellers was rigidly applied by M&S in the days before open displays when much of the stock was on island "L" shaped counters. As men's shirts and women's knitwear were proven good sellers, they would invariably be featured on counters at the front of the store with the best selling lines promoted on the "front end".

The second option takes an opposing view and assumes that the demand product will sell wherever it is positioned. Hence, lower yielding departments such as books and footwear are placed at the front of shop. A particular advantage of this option is that customers, when heading for the demand product, will be forced to pass stock displays not usually encountered and additional sales may result.

On a similar theme, food supermarkets make themselves unpopular by constantly changing the location of their food categories – just as the customer had remembered where everything was, they find the following week it's all changed around. This is a deliberate ploy by supermarkets to ensure that in the quest to locate a basic line along an unfamiliar route, the hapless customer may discover and hopefully buy a new product!

Charity shops may apply the same technique but the advantages are lessened, as in comparison, our shops are so compact that what we have to offer is usually evident from the outset.

One final point - it makes sense to display high value items within view of the counter rather than out of sight in a dark corner!

Counters

Another consideration is where to position the all-important counter. One recommended best position (when viewed from the outside looking in) is on the right-hand-side at the front of the shop. The reasoning being that according to some research, people when entering a room, tend to progress in a clockwise direction. Were the counter placed on the other side, it would be a barrier deterring further exploration – as people tend to shy away from a point of authority.

This logic may seem a little spurious and one wonders whether it would apply to shops in the Southern Hemisphere where it is a known fact that water draining from a plug hole rotates in the opposite direction – does this also mean that Antipodeans progress anti-clockwise when entering a room? Whatever, there are sounder grounds for siting the counter at the front, albeit left or right – that is for security reasons as customers, having to pass the counter on exiting, are less likely to leave without paying!

Finally, wherever counters are sited, they should afford a good view of all parts of the shops. Glass-fronted units are useful for securely displaying valuable items of jewellery and ornaments etc. Furthermore, counters should not be bigger than is absolutely necessary to accommodate a till, fold purchases and display counter-promoted information and goods. An unnecessarily large counter, particularly in a small shop, absorbs valuable display space.

Fitting Rooms

Also referred to as changing rooms, these are essential for any clothing shop and especially for those selling used items where the declared size may no longer be accurate.

They are best positioned in the less productive areas of the shop usually at the rear or, where appropriate, under a staircase leading to an upper floor. A full–length mirror should be provided which should be sealed around the edges to prevent unscrupulous customers from removing and concealing price tickets. One inventive charity used a mirror above which was printed: "Are you looking at our next shop volunteer?"

Further guidance on fitting rooms and their compliance with the requirements of the Disability Discrimination Act is given in the Association of Charity Shops' Members' Handbook.

Display Methods & Equipment

A comprehensive description of all the display methods and equipment available is beyond the scope of this section.

Reference to the many equipment catalogues available will show the extensive products obtainable and a list of possible suppliers can also be viewed on the Association of Charity Shops' website.

The following covers the principal considerations for this topic.

Versatility

As previously mentioned, our stock in trade comprises mainly of clothing supplemented by a range of bric-a–brac items. **An essential requirement of a good charity shopfit is that it has the flexibility to accommodate the unpredictable and ever-changing range and quantity of donations received.** For example, a shop manager suddenly overrun with a new donation of good bric-a-brac must be able to quickly convert a metre-run of clothing rail to shelving.

The standard method of displaying clothing in charity shops is on wall-mounted rails and freestanding floor rails. The former are usually attached to "U"-sectioned slotted steel uprights screwed to the wall at one-metre centres. This system is available in various finishes and obtainable from a variety of suppliers. Its versatility allows any number of shelf/rail combinations to be quickly slotted into place.

Rails are available in a variety of shapes ranging from straight to "D" shaped and combination rails which include an arm protruding at right angles enabling some garments to be featured front-facing. The latter gives a more interesting display than a regimented run of clothing with only the edges visible like books on a shelf.

All this is a far cry from the inflexible fittings of the 1970s where the norm for wall railing was 2"x2" timber uprights spanned by runs of fixed gas pipe. There was very little scope for flexibility in those days!

Similarly, freestanding floor rails are available in a number of designs ranging from circular to the more interesting "Swastika" configuration where four garments fronts can be featured. It should be noted, however, that the more complex the design, the fewer garments can be displayed per square foot.

Special one–metre display grids, shoe shelves, general usage baskets and millinery arms are also available within the system.

Lighting

A common criticism levelled at charity shops is they are too often badly lit. Too many are illuminated by banks of sombre strip-lights with diffusers full of dead flies. The impact from a row of halogen spotlights is enormous and especially when directed onto wall displays. Charities are often reluctant to invest in adequate lighting as they feel it is unnecessary expenditure. Admittedly running costs will be higher but this is more than offset by the improved ambience, which attracts customers, promotes the merchandise and increases its perceived value.

Floor Coverings

Following the current trend in commercial shops, more and more charity shops are fitting laminated floors in preference to the more traditional carpet. Such floors are harder-wearing, odour-proof, stain-proof and arguably easier to keep clean – what's more they convey a more modern and up-market image. Whatever covering is chosen, it is important that a neutral colour is selected so as not to compete with the multitude of colour already inherent in second hand clothing. Where carpet is the choice, consider using carpet tiles as they can be uplifted and transferred to a new shop and easily replaced where there is heavy wear or staining etc.

Coat Hangers

More appropriately termed garment hangers, these are available in a variety of materials, colours and type. The wire ones, so beloved of dry-cleaners, should be avoided as they support very little weight and, when stored, soon become a tangled mess! Many charities select a colour to conform to their charity house colour – be aware, however, that strong colours (particularly red) can make the hangers appear more dominant than the merchandise! So much so that one frustrated area manager is reported to have commented: "what are we selling here, women's tops or red coat hangers?" Neutral grey, black or white show off the merchandise to best advantage.

There are special hangers available for items such as skirts, trousers and household linen – the latter having a wide cross bar and fabricated from thick gauge wire necessary to support the weight of heavy curtains etc.

By Size or Colour?

A frequently debated topic amongst charity shop managers is whether to display clothing ranges by size or by colour, the latter being known as 'colour-blocking'. Undoubtedly the most visually pleasing is colour-blocking with some enlightened shops graduating their displays from red through violet following the colours of the spectrum – the impact here can be breathtaking!

The method to adopt depends on your view of whether the potential customer's priority is first to seek out size followed by colour or colour followed by size. Alternatively, some consider that price takes precedence, though there are few charity shops that group by price.

On balance, it is probably best to display by size and restrict colour-blocking to big impact new shop opening days or for established up-market locations which command higher prices and where there are enough volunteers to cope with the extra work involved.

Footwear

Nothing deteriorates as quickly as shoes as they take more than their fair share of everyday wear and tear. Hence, compared with clothing, the proportion that can be salvaged for resale is low.

They are best displayed on custom wire shoe shelves slotted into the wall uprights. Their value is enhanced if trouble is taken to polish them as not only do they look better but also the smell of Cherry Blossom polish adds appeal.

To reduce stock losses, many charities display footwear in singles with the partner shoe kept in the stockroom.

Books

Books can be a very lucrative product for charity shops as in relation to the space they occupy they have a high re-sale value –

what's more, they are infinitely recyclable with many purchased books returning as donations! They are invariably placed on shelves and are best grouped by category especially where there is an enthusiastic volunteer who makes books their special responsibility.

Although usually displayed with the spines upright, some shops lay them on their side arguing that by so doing, the titles can more easily be read and more books can be accommodated by filling the space right up to the shelf above.

Cash Collection Units

The permanent presence of a charity shop offers a good opportunity to collect cash donations via both counter collection boxes and the larger floor-standing ones. Combined annual income from such units can be as high as £2,000, a very useful addition to income, which does not sacrifice display space, and directly attracts the very commodity a charity wants – cash!

Where possible the floor-standing unit should be placed outside on the pavement where it will attract extra donations from passers-by. However, it is worth checking with the local authority, as some will perceive this as an obstruction to the pavement. Shops having a recessed entrance are ideally placed. To prevent theft, the unit should be chained to a suitable fixing and brought in at night. The units with a clear domed top where coins spiral downwards in a vortex are particularly effective and have the added advantage of having no moving parts and requiring no mains electricity to operate them.

Window Displays

The shop window provides the all-important first impression of what is to be found inside and a good one will convert passers-by into customers. The impact must be immediate as you only have a few seconds to grab the attention of the potential punter.

Detailed information on planning and building an effective display is beyond the scope of this guide. However, here are a few important reminders:

- Make it appropriate for the time of year

- Do not clutter

- Keep it simple using a maximum of two colour schemes

- Create a focal point

- Use appropriate accessories to enhance the display

- Featured items should be boldly priced

Much can be learnt and applied from checking out the displays of high street fashion retailers and there is often a volunteer who has a talent for display who will be enthusiastic to take responsibility for the window.

4

Pricing

The Fixed-Costs Effect

Perhaps the most difficult, yet important task for a charity shop manager is setting the optimum selling price for the varied range and condition of the items donated. Unlike other second-hand goods there are no pricing guides for clothing to refer to - there is no equivalent of Glass's Guide (motor trade) or Miller's Guide (antiques).

That being the case, the shop manager cannot know whether that *Next*-labelled, in fashion, two-piece suit in pristine condition and selling new at £75, is worth £12 or £20. However, under or over-estimating its value will have a significant impact on net profitability.

This is illustrated by the following simplified example based on the **annual performance** of a typical shop:

Sales	£ 100,000
Running costs	£ 80,000
Net contribution	**£ 20,000**

Increasing selling prices by 10%, the revised outcome is as follows:

Sales	£ 110,000
Running costs	£ 80,000
Net contribution	**£ 30,000**

Consequently, an increase of just 10% in income results in 50% more profit. Specifically, it means that women's tops originally sold at £2.25 would be increased to £2.50 and 50p ties to 55p – Hardly significant increases when compared with the original new price of these items!

For a shop chain with a net contribution of £1m, a 10% hoist in income means an extra £500,000 profit – or, for the sample of the sector covered by the Charity Finance survey, a massive £47m extra!

This dramatic uplift in profit from a small increase in sales is a unique feature of charity shop retailing – this is because, generally speaking, **running costs remain fixed regardless of sales.**

Conversely, a commercial retailer increasing income by 10% must lay out more money for purchases and will probably have to take on more sales staff to manage the extra business. In our case the stock and labour is provided free, a considerable and unique advantage!

Depreciation

A particular drawback for our sector is that the stock we are given has a relatively low re-sale value – an average of only £2-£4, per item. This is because our stock comprises mainly used clothing and nothing depreciates faster than that!

For instance, a man's suit in pristine condition, currently selling new at £150, donated on the day of purchase may well be priced at £30 in a well–fitted and well-positioned charity shop – that's just 20% of its value new. Compare that with the re-sale value of a car, which might fetch 80% of its purchase price if sold within a month of purchase. Furthermore, a house is likely to sell for more that its original cost. Even faster-depreciating jewellery, furniture and electronic goods in "as new" condition will probably realise half their value.

Setting the Price

A national chain of commercial shops will usually operate a uniform pricing structure. This is not feasible for charity shops as no two items are alike and, besides in our case, there are unique factors that influence price:

Competition: This includes other charity shops as well as commercial 'value' clothing retailers

Shopfit: The quality of the shopfit by way of equipment and lighting etc. will have a bearing on the perceived value of the stock

Stock inflow: To maximise throughput and ultimate sales and profit, a shop that receives large donations of quality stock may deliberately price on the low side – 100 items sold at £2 is more profitable than 50 items sold at £2.50. This strategy only makes sense for our sector where stock is free of charge. It would be a different matter if we had to pay!

Local economy: Certain items can be priced-up in affluent areas – Whereas that designer outfit might sell at £35 in a Home Counties up-market town, it might only fetch £15 in a less affluent location. Some charities operating large chains transfer stock between shops to get maximum value.

There is a tendency for some managers to under-price as they want to be popular with the customers – a comment like "I much prefer to shop here as compared with the charity shop across the road your prices are so reasonable" will undoubtedly bring a smug glow of satisfaction, but, it might be that the competition's higher prices actually make more money for its parent charity.

Setting prices for charity shops is an art not a science. A good manager knows better than anyone what is the right level for her/his shop.

Effects of Inflation

High inflation poses a potential threat to our sector. Happily, in recent years we have benefited from relatively low inflation of around 3% p.a. However, in the late 1970s this peaked at over 20% when, because of the intuitive nature of our pricing, charities did not increase prices to compensate. The effect of this was that, whilst operating costs were racing ahead, income remained static and profit was severely eroded.

Whereas a commercial retailer can counter inflation and maintain margin by adding a fixed percentage mark-up to a supplier's invoice, we have no such mechanism. If, in a previous year, volunteers had priced a shirt at £2.50, they might not spontaneously adjust to £3.00. After all, they are not machines that can be programmed!

Consistency

Having too many pricers will usually result in inconsistent pricing and a wide span of prices for similar items – this is both annoying and confusing for the customer. It is not unusual for the "Thursday" volunteer pricer to disagree with her "Wednesday" counterpart and set about changing them up or down!

It is recommended that just one person in the shop be given responsibility for pricing. This is usually the manager whose involvement may simply be to write the price on a previously prepared and attached price ticket.

Compassionate Pricing

Many customers believe charity shops are too greedy asking inflated prices for their stock. A common comment is: "Why are you charging so much, after all, the stock was given to you in the first place". Similarly, because of our charity status, there is sometimes an expectation that we should dispense charity in its own right by discounting or giving away clothing to 'needy' individuals.

When challenged, managers can respond by emphasising the following:

- The shop exists to raise as much money as possible for the charity it supports – it was not set up to provide cheap clothing for the community.
- The seemingly high prices are entirely justified as:

- The shop has to pay rent, rates, light and heat and other running costs. Despite being a charity, these are not provided free!
- Many donors expect their donation to be realistically priced as they want to give maximum benefit to the charity – to price too low is often an insult.

Pricing Guides

Many charities produce pricing guides. These are usually fixed to stockroom walls for reference. Generally these guides indicate price-ranges for typical clothing items designated *poor, good* and *excellent* condition etc. Some charities will categorise their shops into bands with pricing ranges appropriate for each band. Guides have their uses but, given the variety of stock we are given, deciding the level of condition is somewhat subjective. They are probably more appropriate for new or inexperienced staff that, once "into the job", are more likely to apply intuitive prices based on their knowledge of the area i.e. what is in demand and what people are prepared to pay.

Half-Price Sales

Some charity shops feature a run of "Half Marked Price" clothing. The discounted items are often stock that has reached its stock rotation expiry date and is being given a last chance of sale before ragging – or it might be a clearance of last season's stock.

The acid test for gauging the effectiveness of discounted stock is whether or not it brings overall additional sales. Some argue that it is ineffective to sell items at reduced prices when the space could be more productively used to sell full-price items. It is not as if we are trying to recover purchase costs - the clothing was donated in the first place!

In deciding whether to sell reduced stock we should also take into account the promotional value of a sale rail. If well promoted, it may add new interest to the shop bringing new customers. On balance however, price reductions are probably more appropriate for shops that are not overrun with lots of quality donations – where they are, it is surely better to get full price on everything!

Like so much in charity retail, it is worth experimenting to see what works for you.

Valuable Items

Despite the effect of "money in the attic" type programmes and the growing popularity of online auction houses such as eBay, charity shops continue to receive quite valuable donations including rare books, paintings and jewellery. The trick is to spot these treasures before the customer does! Many an item of jewellery or porcelain has been bought for a few pounds only to realise thousands for the lucky buyer at auction.

Shop managers and volunteers cannot be expected to be knowledgeable about value for the great assortment of books and bric-a-brac we are given. But, they should have a talent or 'nose' for spotting what **might** be valuable – such items being put aside for valuation by a trusted expert who is often the local antique dealer or auction house. Furthermore, charity shops can 'phone through to Sotheby's or other respected auction houses for advice.

Understandably, customers do not always have the confidence to pay a charity shop, say, £300 for a diamond solitaire. So, valuable items are best sold to the local antique shop or via an auction house, albeit that some commission may be charged, though some auctioneers waive or discount this for charities. Where high-value items are displayed in the shop, they are more likely to sell if they are exhibited alongside an independent valuation.

It is important that items put aside for valuation are assessed and sold promptly and not allowed to languish for long periods in locked cupboards where they deprive the charity of funds and are more likely to 'go missing'.

Testing Price Levels

No one is really qualified to say whether a charity shop's pricing is too high, too low or about right; yet for reasons already covered, getting the levels right has such a dramatic impact on profit. A good shop manager will periodically test price levels. This is simply done by taking one department at a time. For example, there may be a suspicion that women's trousers are under-priced;

what would be the effect of increasing them by say, 20%? To test this, it will be necessary to record unit sales and income at present prices for a month and then uplift the prices by 20% and monitor for a further month.

The test completed, it may be found that unit sales have decreased by 10% but overall revenue has increased – the test has proved therefore that higher prices for this department will produce more sales and profit. Conversely, where it is felt that a department might be over-priced, prices can be lowered. Providing that the department's revenue is up, this is the way to go.

By changing prices one department at a time there is no risk of damaging the total business as we are assessing the unique pricing tolerance levels of each department. This 'suck it and see' policy is surely better than the all too familiar cry of: "Sales are disappointing, let's increase everything by 10%".

'Psychological' Pricing

The prices in most high street shops end with 99p – e.g. £3.99 or £19.99. In the days before decimalisation, the equivalent was 19s. 11d. It was pitched that way, not only to convey value, but also for security reasons, as it ensured that the sales assistant had to open the till to give change! Because so many people nowadays pay by debit and credit card the security advantage is lessened.

For charity shops, it is likewise recommended to price just below the next whole pound because the suffix 99p or 95p suggests better value. Hence £4.99 is more enticing than £5 and, incidentally, more profitable than £4.95 - demonstrated as follows:

> Assume a typical charity shop with weekly sales of £2,000 and an average unit selling price of £2.50. This shop will be selling 41,600 items per year. Therefore, having a 95p suffix policy rather than 99p, it is losing out on 4p per item sold. **This translates to lost income of £1,664 per year** – perhaps enough to pay the business rates or employ the assistant manager for another 5 hours per week!

So-called psychological pricing can be further refined; for instance, a customer faced with a price of £3.75, may subconsciously round it up to £4 as, after all, it is nearly £4. In that case, why not make it

£4.25, as that too is *"nearly"* £4 though 13% more than the original price of £3.75! Conversely a price of 55p might be regarded as half a pound whereas 70p, though only 15p more, could subconsciously be rounded up to £1 making it appear twice as expensive.

Remember that because of the high level of annual transactions that a charity shop enjoys, **a small adjustment to the average unit-selling price can have a significant impact on profit.**

Further Tips

- Ensure that all items are ticketed with the price boldly marked. Many charities use large tickets for window merchandise so that details can easily be read from outside the shop.

- Copies of an Argos catalogue, appropriate mail-order catalogues and Miller's Guide etc. should be kept in the stockroom as a reference for pricing. Checking the prices bid for items listed on eBay can also be a useful guide for pricing.

- Clothing with exclusive fashion labels can be marked up in price and promoted using special tickets such as "Labels for Less" or "Bargain Brand names" etc.

5

Stock Generation

A regular in-flow of stock donations is the life-blood of any charity shop. Enormous quantities are required to keep the rails and shelves full. A typical shop turning over £1,500 per week will sell approximately 30,000 items per year and, assuming that 75% of all donations are rejected as unsuitable for display, it will need to attract and process four times that volume – that's 120,000 items!

Fortunately, due to the long-accepted concept of charity shops in the UK, the general public is aware of our needs and continues to provide enough stock to fulfil the requirements of the estimated 7,500 shops. Though not wishing to diminish the altruistic motives in making donations, there is nonetheless a two-way benefit as our shops also provide a convenient means of discarding unwanted items – especially if they are collected through house-to-house collections.

Whilst the sector is forever grateful for the support it receives, there is nonetheless a frustration that, in general, it cannot influence the content of stock it receives – a manager desperate for large sizes but overwhelmed with size 8s, 10s and 12s must surely envy their commercial counterparts who can place an order to replenish particular items of stock. Nevertheless, this inconvenience is a small price to pay for the considerable advantage of low or nil cost of sales.

Sources of Supply

Direct Donations

In an ideal world, all the stock needed would be brought directly to the shop. There would be no need for donation appeals or costly house-to-house stock collections to organise. In the real world however, if charity shops are to exploit their full potential, they must supplement 'over-the-door' donations with extra supplies. Although the pioneering shops of the 1960s and 1970s traded profitably on entirely directly-donated stock, there is no doubt that overall sales and profits would have been higher had they adopted present stock generation initiatives.

Poster Appeals

Although the constant requirement for donated stock is generally appreciated, there is no harm in constantly reminding people. The most obvious approach is to appeal for stock via posters displayed in the shop window and around the shop.

Whilst the sector is trying to get across that it wants unwanted clothing and bric-a-brac, this general message can be conveyed in a variety of inventive guises: "Free up your wardrobe and cupboard space...", "Don't bin it, bring it!", "Don't rate it? Donate it!"

Where there are specific stock needs, posters can be modified to appeal for particular donations such as old cameras, costume jewellery or men's suits etc. Such prompts often trigger off a response; for instance, mentioning cameras might remind a passer-by that the family have all updated to digital and have several old film cameras lying around unloved and unused! A general stock appeal may not have brought the same response.

Posters can also be used to appeal for shop equipment such as vacuum cleaners, irons and even computers – if you don't ask you don't get!

Customers

Though not practiced nearly enough, a direct appeal to customers can be very effective. On completing a sale at the counter, why not make a simple and politely given request such as: "I hope you will be pleased with your purchase and please think of us next time you are having a clear out – all the stock in this shop has been donated in this way".

Volunteers

Apart from their important contribution of time and effort, volunteers can also be a valuable source of donations. A shop with say 20 active volunteers will not only contribute stock in their own right, but may also influence their families, friends and neighbours to support the shop where they work – thus 20 volunteers might mean 100 or more potential stock donators.

Local Traders

Many shop managers have successfully approached local shopkeepers for unwanted stock or for raffle prizes. Usually this is by means of a simple appeals letter written on the charity's headed paper. Even 'big name' national retailers are happy to help out, especially when their national policy is to support the local community.

Corporates

The vast majority of stock donations received in charity shops originate from a domestic source, be it a direct donation or one generated via house-to-house collections. Yet potentially there are mountains of suitable and unwanted stock lying about in warehouses and offices throughout the UK. Many charities have had considerable success in attracting these donations. Specifically, the items available will be described in the trade as:

- Soiled and damaged
- End of line
- Customer returns
- Out of season
- Rep's samples
- Staff work-wear and uniforms
- Redundant promotional items

A carefully selected array of companies can be approached by letter and later followed up by a phone call. It is important that the approach also emphasises the benefits to the donor company i.e. a chance to free-up valuable storage space, reclaim VAT and an opportunity for recognition by acknowledging the donation thus - "These items have kindly been donated by XYZ plc". Understandably, many companies insist that any branding be removed before sale so as not to elicit complaints over quality and refund requests etc.

Using this approach, one charity received thousands of navy blue two-piece suits from a national airline, which, due to an updated design, were redundant air stewardess' uniforms. These were quickly snapped up by young women wanting a smart and inexpensive outfit for work and the donation made tens of thousands of pounds. Similarly, a national retailer donated their redundant sales assistants' overalls, which sold in their thousands as housecoats.

Redundant promotional items such as t-shirts, sweatshirts and promotional gifts (pens, watches and calculators etc.) can also be very lucrative.

Even if clothing items do not all sell, they have a value as textile waste.

Once an initial donation is forthcoming, it is good practice to let the donor know how much money has been made and attempt to establish an on-going relationship so that the company contacts your charity every time it has surplus stock.

Bear in mind the saleability of some of the donations may be dubious, as the 'cream' may well have already been offered to the staff or sold to market traders etc. Accordingly, where appropriate, it is advisable to ask for a sample before committing to a lorry load. Additionally, it can help if you offer to arrange collection from the company's premises.

For larger charities with specialist Corporate Fundraising Departments it is best to keep that department informed of the companies you intend to contact, as you do not want to confuse and annoy the supporter with an uncoordinated approach. You might even ask your Corporate Fundraising Department or equivalent to mention the shop's stock needs when they talk to their corporate supporters.

House-to-House Collections (Bag Drops)

The introduction of house-to–house collections by many charities in the early 1980s has probably had more impact on sales than any other initiative. Charity shops are no longer dependent for their stock on what is brought directly – they can, in theory, go out and collect unlimited supplies of stock. Additionally, householders benefit from this cost-free clearance service as they no longer have to lug heavy bags of stock to their local shop. Such a convenient way of giving ensures that more stock is made available to charity shops than solely relying on direct-to-shop donations. House-to-house collections of goods by charities, are, however, regulated in England, Wales and Northern Ireland. Charities must be authorized to carry out these collections either by holding a national exemption order or a license from the relevant local authority.

For many charity shop chains the major part of their sales now originate from collected stock with some charities' dependence being as high as 70%-80%. Predictably, these benefits bring additional costs, which can be substantial. For many dependent chains this is their largest operating cost after staff costs and property costs. Much of the sector's diminished profit margin is a direct result.

How It Works

Basically, a plastic sack inserted into a charity-branded plastic envelope is distributed for subsequent collection. There are a number of specialist manufactures that supply the materials as well as providing help with the design.

Essentially, the envelope should include brief details of the charity's work, its registered charity number, a list of the items sought and notification of when the sack will be collected. The latter is usually indicated by circling a specific day from a pre-printed list of days of the week. **To avoid frustration and uphold the reputation of the charity, it is very important that the declared collection date is adhered to.**

There are several options over who is used to undertake the sack distribution and collection. The best option being volunteer collectors, though, for practical reasons, few charities rely on volunteers entirely to carry out this time-consuming and often tiring work. Accordingly, most will use either self-employed staff or directly employed collectors. Where self-employed staff are used, measures should be taken to ensure that the agreed duties undertaken qualify for self-employment status, so as not to fall foul of taxation and employment law. Professional advice should be sought on this.

Whatever is decided, it is imperative that collectors are issued with and carry a signed collection authority which for reasons of security, should be time-limited – usually renewable quarterly. Additionally, the staff should be smart and courteous and the vehicles used clean and in good condition.

Remember that collection teams are representing your charity and a poor image will potentially tarnish its reputation.

Regulation

Charities carrying out significant levels of collections in England, Wales and Northern Ireland may apply for an Exemption Order (currently issued in England and Wales by the Home Office). Under the House-to-House Collections Act, they must make an annual return to the Home Office declaring the income derived and expenses incurred on these collections. As such it is necessary for the sales of collected stock to be separately recorded and records kept of all associated expenses.

In any event, these records are vital for the charity itself to monitor the contribution made by these collections. Additionally, records should be kept to include information on response rates i.e. the percentage of sacks returned both full and empty. There is provision to record this information in the *Collection Sack Information* box on the suggested *Weekly Report* within this guide's section on *Basic Shop Administration and Reporting.*

Smaller charities that operate locally or regionally must apply to the relevant local authority for a license to carry out collections. Local authorities differ in the way they deal with such requests and the period for which they will grant permission for such collections to take place.

The regulations covering charity fundraising, including house-to-house collections are under review in England and Wales as part of the development of the new Charities Act but these are unlikely to come into effect until 2007 at the earliest. In Scotland, the collection of goods by charities is currently unregulated although this is also under review as part of the new charities legislation that has been implemented north of the border.

More comprehensive information on the techniques of running an efficient house-to-house collection operation is beyond the scope of this guide.

Bogus Collections

Unfortunately, there are many bogus collectors operating whose literature misleadingly infers that the appeal supports charity whereas only a small percentage or none is allocated. Sadly, theft of charity collections sacks does also take place. To reduce the incidence of sham operators it is recommended that charities report any suspicious collections to the local authority and also involve the police, if there is evidence of theft of the charity's donations. The Association of Charity Shops also keeps records of such collections to help build up evidence against these unscrupulous and damaging operators.

Textile Banks

In the late 1980s many charities took advantage of the government's new directive for local authorities to recycle more domestic waste. Enterprising charities seized the initiative by placing branded textile collection banks on council amenity sites and supermarket car parks etc. Although most of the available sites have now been taken by three major charity shop chains, there are still opportunities for more placements.

The banks are available from a number of specialist manufacturers. In most cases a contract is drawn up with a local textile merchant to clear the contents for an agreed rate per tonne collected. Such merchants are often the same ones used to clear accumulations of the charity's shop generated rag. It should be noted that recent legislation now makes it obligatory for merchants undertaking this work to carry a *Waste Carrier's Licence*.

Alternatively, where a bank is sited near an existing shop and it is practical for the contents to be cleared by the shop's staff or van driver, suitable items can be sold directly through the shop. This arrangement is, of course, much more profitable as **the value of**

used clothing sold through a shop is approximately 40 times greater than its value as textile waste.

By way of further development in this area, some charities are also placing specially designed banks for the collection of books and shoes.

Guidance on good practice and regulatory requirements for house-to-house collections and banks is provided in the Association of Charity Shops' Members' Handbook.

Place of Work and School Collections

Factories and offices can be a productive source of stock. Permission is sought to leave a supply of collection sacks in a reception area or staff canteen etc., with the filled sacks being collected after an agreed period.

It helps if the management or head teacher gets behind the appeal encouraging the staff/pupils to support it. Such collections can be very profitable as they are usually a very low-cost/high-response activity compared with a more costly and less productive house-to-house collection.

A possible catalyst for these collections may be a stock appeal following a talk on the work of the charity to staff or pupils.

Unclaimed Lost Property

It is worthwhile, periodically, to approach transport companies and local authorities for unclaimed lost property – it's surprising how many watches, rings and mobile phones are left on bus seats and in changing cubicles at public swimming baths!

Some Reminders

Try Not To Refuse Stock

Some charity shops have been known to turn donations away because they are overwhelmed with stock or they deem it to be of unsuitable quality. This can be very insulting to the donor and will usually force them to transfer their allegiance to another charity.

If storage space is a problem then arrangements can often be made for temporary storage in a lock-up garage or the erection of a garden shed in an area behind the shop. Alternatively, where there are neighbouring shops, the stock can be transferred. Even if the quality is dubious, remember that nearly all textiles have a value as rag. Inevitably, however, charities will be justified in rejecting bulky unsaleable items such as mattresses, prams and mains electrical goods etc

Always Say 'Thank-You'

It's surprising how many donors who walk into a shop with a bag of donations are greeted with either no response at all or a curt comment like; "Leave it there"! Even worse is when, whilst the donor is still in the shop, the 'behind the counter' team, set about rummaging through the bag making comments such as: "That's for the rag bag", "This will fit your Janet, Elsie" and "I think I'll have that one".

A heart-felt and sincere 'thank you' does wonders and will influence the supporter to choose that shop again for future donations.

Like Attracts Like

The quality of stock that a shop receives is often related to the quality and price demanded for the stock on display – the better the quality and more realistic the price, the better the donations. Understandably, donors want their donation to realise as much money for the charity as possible and will be put off by a shop, which priced their last pristine, in-vogue outfit donation for £3.99 when it must have been worth at least £10!

Smell

An often-quoted reason for not using charity shops is that all too often they are spoilt by a lingering and pervasive smell of old clothes – there is no bigger turn off for the potential customer. Rogue sacks where damp clothes have been stored are often the cause of the problem. Strangely, the staff who work on the premises are usually unaware of the these off-putting aromas – perhaps, this is because they have become a too familiar part of the shop's ambience and go unnoticed in the same way that 'doggy' smells in dog-owning households are only noticed by visitors.

To keep the shop smelling sweet, it is recommended that there are frequent squirts from an aerosol air freshener or an investment in an automatic battery-powered dispenser where the spray intervals can be preset.

6

Stock Preparation and Disposal

The Stockroom

The stockroom is, in effect, the engine room of a charity shop. It must be organised and managed efficiently if it is to effectively process the vast quantities of stock received annually. A shop with a turnover of £2,000 per week is likely to process approximately 170,000 donated items annually - that's more than one per minute, quite a production line!

The 'perfect' charity shop would have a stockroom with a minimum of 300 square feet situated at ground level immediately behind the sales floor. Many shops, however, operate successfully with smaller areas and less than ideal locations in basements, upper floors or even outside sheds etc.

It is also an advantage to have separate rear access as this helps when receiving large stock donations and clearing rags.

An efficient stockroom will include:

Sorting Table – This should be large and custom-built and preferably with a surface measuring 8'x4' and a work top height of 3'. Many shops attempt to make do with an old kitchen or dining room table – at approx 2.5' high, this is too low making it awkward and tiring to work at for long periods, especially for the usually elderly volunteer sorters.

A Rag Pen – Unsorted clothing and rag stored in polythene sacks can be very difficult to control as, like wet fish, they slide about all over the floor! An ideal solution is a 'rag pen' which is a cage built usually from soft wood, compartmentalised and spanning from floor to ceiling.

Sack Frames – Limp sacks are notoriously difficult to fill! Far better to support the sacks on one of the many sack frames/supports available, some of which are designed for bagging garden waste and are available from garden centres and ironmongers etc.

Wall Rails And Shelves – For ease of access and to keep them fresh, stocks of out-of-season and back-up clothing are best hung on rails. Likewise, bric-a-brac should be placed on shelves rather than stacked up on the floor in cardboard boxes.

Recently processed stock, deemed fit for sale, is usually hung on a portable rail in readiness for pricing and transfer to the sales floor.

Steamer – Although not generally used by charity shops until the late 1970s, a steamer has become an indispensable piece of equipment replacing the less productive iron and ironing-board. Not only does a steamer quickly freshen up and remove creases from a garment, it is also effective at removing small stains, meaning that a percentage of items are saved from the ragbag.

Some shops have speeded up the process by steaming against a padded surface fixed to a wall or door back – this means that a garment's front and back can be steamed simultaneously.

Washing Machines – Although a washing-machine is another option for enhancing stock, the large number of items that would require washing and drying plus higher running costs renders this choice less practical than steamers, though some shops do have one installed. Alternatively, many shops have volunteers prepared to take clothing home to be washed in the family machine.

Tagging Gun – A quick and efficient way to attach a price ticket to a garment. The gun is 'loaded' with a strip of plastic attachments, which are 'shot' through the ticket and garment together providing a firm fixing. Prior to tagging guns, those charity shops, which were bothering to pre-price, used either pins or an office stapler – the latter ruining many a delicate fabric!

Stock 'Gauge' – An effective way to maintain maximum stock density on the sales-floor is for the hangers from sold items to be quickly returned to the stockroom. These are placed on a prominently placed 'Stock Gauge' rail and subsequently re-hung with a replacement garment, which is returned to the sales floor. Consequently, 25 hangers on the 'Gauge' rail will give an immediate indication that the shop is 25 items short of maximum capacity meaning a potential loss of sales.

Sizing Cubes – These are another 1970s innovation and are simply a coloured cube indicating size and affixed to a hanger. Hence, a customer on the lookout for size 16, can head directly for the yellow cubes, without having to scrutinise each label.

Stock Rotation

Like house-to-house collections and professional shopfits, the introduction of stock rotation in the mid 1970s had a dramatic and immediate impact on sales. In essence, it is a means of giving every displayed item a shelf-life after which it is removed from display.

In retrospect, stock rotation was a fairly obvious innovation recognising that if an item were desirable it would sell quickly. After all, there is no logic in continuing to display slow selling stock when, being donated, there are no purchase costs to recover and replacement supplies are waiting in the stockroom.

Prior to stock rotation, stock was allowed to 'rot on the rails' with some items remaining on display for many months or even years!

Duration

Dependent on the levels of stock received, **the rotation period normally ranges from one week to six weeks but is usually set between two and three weeks.**

A shop which receives lots of quality over-the-door donations and/or productive house-to-house collections will normally operate a short rotation period as it will have a generous pool of stock from which to replenish the time-expired and culled stock.

Whilst short rotation periods result in a smaller proportion of the displayed stock being sold, it will usually bring higher overall sales. This is because more desirable items sell quickly and by refreshing the stock frequently, the shop will be able to offer a greater proportion of desirable, quick selling items.

To fulfil the greater stock needs required, a short rotation period also means that house-to-house collections usually have to be increased. This, of course, incurs extra costs and **managers should monitor whether increased overall sales actually result in more profit.**

Shops which are less well supported with stock, usually operate a longer rotation period. Here, a greater proportion of the stock is sold and there are lower stock collection costs, but lower total sales probably mean less profit.

In summary: **short rotation periods usually mean more profit** but they can only be used where there is sufficient stock!

The item's expiry date is usually written on the ticket as either a date or a week number (found in most diaries). The latter is preferable as an exact date might prompt a wily customer to wait another week knowing it will be marked down to half price!

Some charity shops use a different coloured tag attachment to signify the stock's expiry date. Hence, all items first displayed on a particular week will all have the same coloured attachment – so, for example, a shop operating a three-week rotation period might tag goods displayed during w/c 1st January with red attachments with that stock being taken off during w/c 22nd January.

A Second Chance

Time-expired stock is usually put in the ragbag and sold as textile waste. However, some charities attempt to clear more by offering it at half price for another two weeks or so, a topic covered in the earlier chapter on *Pricing*.

Alternatively, where a charity runs other shops in the vicinity, the stock may be given a second chance in a new location. Where this is possible there are usually different coloured sacks kept in the stockroom to identify Stock Transfers - these are regularly collected and distributed by the area manager or equivalent.

Rag Disposal

Charity shops are big generators of rag or "textile waste" as it is now called. Quantities originate from a combination of clothing stock rejected for sale plus items that have passed their stock rotation expiry date. Most shops will accumulate several tonnes per year with the charity shop sector being a major source of supply.

Payment Methods

A textile merchant generally clears the waste weekly and will have a variety of payment methods:

- On-the-spot payment at an agreed average price per sack

- On-the-spot payment at an agreed price per tonne with the sacks being weighed on a spring balance carried on the merchant's vehicle

- At an agreed price per tonne but payment made later based on the weights recorded back at the merchant's premises.

More detailed information on good practice and regulations for safe waste disposal is available in the Association of Charity Shops' Members' Handbook.

Uses for Charity Rag

Until the early 1980s most of the waste collected from charity shops was used for recycling into new textiles or for use as industrial wiping cloths. Wool was the most sought-after waste as it could be broken down and re-dyed with the yarn re-knitted into new garments. White was the most desirable colour because it could be dyed to any colour with black being the least in demand and of lowest value.

Before the advent of synthetic cleaning cloths, cotton and cotton/polyester rag were de-buttoned, cut into squares, packed into boxes and sold to engineering companies etc. for use as wiping cloths. Synthetic materials, brassieres and girdles were of least value being collectively known as "low rag" and sold for the manufacture of roofing felt and upholstery filling etc.

Whilst this trade continues today on a smaller scale, most of the value of charity rag now comes from the clothing that can be pulled out as complete garments for sale to overseas markets. This market was not developed until the 1980s when, as a consequence, there was a dramatic hike in the value of textile waste from which both merchants and charities benefited.

A large merchant will often have premises in a redundant mill and will sort the clothing element of the charity rag into perhaps 30 different grades to satisfy the unique requirements of his overseas markets. For instance, cotton shirts and shorts might be destined for the sunny climes of Nigeria whilst warm winter coats and jumpers will be sent to Pakistan for the colder winters.

It is somewhat satisfying to know that, apart from supporting their charity's cause, charity shops also provide a cheap source of clothing for developing countries, albeit that there are many middle-men making a dollar on the way!

Footwear

Many merchants offer a higher price per tonne for footwear than for textile waste and particularly where they have developed an overseas market. Where this is the case, these items should be separately bagged in pairs for collection by the merchant.

Valuing a Reliable Service

A good textile merchant should not only pay a competitive rate for the waste collected but also provide a prompt and reliable collection service. An accumulation of uncleared rags is not only unsightly but is also a health and safety hazard if it overflows into walkways or obstructs fire exits.

There will be occasions when a competing merchant will offer a higher price and it is tempting to change merchants. But, if the service you are receiving is a good one do not automatically sever the relationship for the sake of a few extra pounds. Often the higher price is a temporary arrangement to attract supplies to satisfy an urgent overseas order – it may soon drop back. It is usually better to inform your existing merchant that a higher price has been offered and invite him to increase his price or stick with him at the present price knowing that you are getting a reliable service.

Volatile Market

Prices for textile waste are notoriously volatile and unpredictable ranging over recent years from a low of £20 per tonne to £300 per tonne. Like so many markets, prices are affected by prevailing dollar strength and the availability of cheaper supplies from other countries. Accordingly, when budgeting, charities should not assume that current prices will be sustained – you can always ask your merchant for predictions on the way the market is going.

7

Basic Shop Administration and Reporting

Like any business handling goods and cash, it is important that charity shops maintain and report critical records of performance. These need not be complicated but should be sufficient to verify cash transactions and provide key data essential for monitoring the business and highlighting areas of concern.

The constant analysis of performance is a necessary discipline for charity shops, as they are particularly vulnerable to internal theft.

Just as the tangible aspects of charity shop retailing have evolved over recent years with the introduction of sophisticated shopfits, stock processing and stock-generation methods, so too have the administration and management controls.

Whereas for years the sector got by with the most rudimentary control procedures, the more experienced and professional senior managers who have now joined the sector have introduced more sophisticated systems. As a result, charity shop operations have become less amateur and more controlled and monitored – and rightly so.

Though many of the new systems are essential and perhaps long overdue, we must be careful not to over-burden our shops' staff with too much paper work. After all, a good manager's time and effort is best deployed generating and sorting stock, recruiting and motivating volunteers and talking with customers rather than toiling at a makeshift desk in a remote corner of a busy stock room.

When a shop manager is taken to task for out-of-date stock, half-empty rails and a stock pen brimming with unsorted sacks, they may well be justified in responding: "Well, once I've finished off the Christmas gift stock count and re-orders, collated the customer survey questionnaires and prepared for my staff appraisal, I might get a chance to manage the shop!"

If shop managers either liked or were good at admin they would more likely be working for the Inland Revenue or an insurance company. The talents we should cherish and exploit most in a shop manager are their organising ability, stock knowledge, customer empathy skills, volunteer motivation, general business sense and the capacity and willingness for hard work.

Obviously it helps if a shop can afford the luxury of a full or even part-time assistant manager, but not all shops can and a good area manager or equivalent will make allowances.

This section does not attempt to provide comprehensive instruction on cash handling and till procedures as such guidance is dependent on the capabilities of the till used and the accounting requirements of individual charities. Accordingly, it is limited to fundamental requirements and considerations.

Stock Losses

A vital check for the efficiency of a commercial retail business is the calculation of stock losses or "shrinkage". This is usually done following an annual stock take and is calculated as follows:

Accounting for Shrinkage

	£ RSP	%
Opening stock	1,000	
Purchases	500	
Stock available for sale	1,500	
Closing stock	300	
Theoretical sales	1,200	
Actual sales receipts	1,175	
Shrinkage	(25)	(2.1%)

Thus, £25 (2.1% of sales) is unaccounted for because of staff/customer theft, refunds and under-ringing. Many retail chains attempt to keep shrinkage below 1%, with 3% and above giving cause for concern.

Regrettably, charity shops cannot calculate shrinkage because they cannot validate the inflow, composition and value of the stock donated – or, as the auditors would say, there is no "audit trail".

Admittedly, systems could be put in place to record the donated items received and their value, but a dishonest manager will simply fail to list an item if its sale proceeds are intended to bypass the charity!

However, where there is cause for concern, some charity shop chains do attempt to calculate stock losses by counting items on the sales floor at the start and end of each week and keeping a daily record of the number of items leaving the stockroom for the sales floor. Hence, covering a week's trading, a stock reconciliation might be summarised as follows:

Weekly Stock Reconciliation

Mon 1st June	Items counted on sales floor – Opening Stock	1,459	a
Mon – Sat	Items leaving stockroom for sales floor	542	b
Sat 6th June	Items counted on sales floor – Closing Stock	1,389	c
	Theoretical unit Sales (a+b-c)	612	d
	Actual unit sales, per till roll	589	e
	Stock loss (e-f)	(23)	f

In the above example it would seem that 23 items are unaccounted for and, like the shrinkage example above, could result from theft and/or under-ringing etc. However, unlike the commercial shrinkage example, there is no guarantee that this is the true position as there is no means of confirming the accuracy of the three stock counts (a,b,c) – an unscrupulous manager can simply 'massage' the values to provide an acceptable result!

In short, whatever safeguards are put in place, we will never be able to track and verify sales arising from the contents of every sack of donated stock.

New entrants to the sector are often surprised to discover that charity shops, having been set up for philanthropic motives, are vulnerable to dishonesty, but sadly they are. Happily, however, the incidence of internal theft is presumed to be low but inevitably it will run to many millions of pounds lost to the sector annually. Accordingly, whilst recognising that we can never eliminate theft, measures should be put in place to reduce it and managers should be alert to the possibilities.

Tills

Tills, also known as cash registers, are now an essential piece of equipment for any charity shop and a far cry from the 1960s and 1970s when many shops used a biscuit tin or drawer for securing cash and recorded sales manually on a piece of paper.

The advent of low price, simple-to-operate and multi-function tills have been a godsend as, apart from being a secure receptacle for the cash, they can perform many useful analytical and security functions, e.g.:

- Analysis of sales by category (menswear, books, women's tops, Christmas cards etc. – useful for monitoring display space allocated – Proportionate Display)
- Calculating average unit sales (in total and by category)
- Calculating customer numbers and average customer spend
- Analysis of takings between specified times (useful when reviewing trading hours and staff cover)
- Producing transaction data for named operators (useful for investigating suspected security problems)

There are a number of till suppliers offering a range of sophistication and prices, right up to an EPOS (Electronic Point of Sale) system where the data is captured and transmitted to a central point for report generation and analysis. Such remote systems relieve the shops staff of time-consuming form filling – as such, many charity chains already have or are considering upgrading their systems.

Credit and Debit Cards

Despite the ever increasing popularity of payment by 'plastic', many charity shops are not yet set up to accept credit and debit cards. This means that they may be losing out on sales. Most shops without the facility will have experienced customers, who having made their purchases and faced with payment of say £20 or more, will not have enough cash on them. Often they will offer to draw cash from a nearby cash dispenser and return – but sadly, many are never seen again with their unclaimed purchases remaining behind the counter!

One charity, having installed card-accepting (PDQ machines) in their shops noticed an immediate uplift in sales of circa £200 per week in their busier shops.

Where no such facilities exist in your shops, seek advice from your bank or charity's Finance Department over how to get started. Although you will incur transaction charges and possible supplementary charges where transaction levels fall below certain minimums, your overall sales and profits could well be higher - careful initial research will indicate whether or not accepting this form of payment is viable for you.

Weekly Report

To effectively monitor the business, it is important that shop managers complete and send to their head office or equivalent a weekly report giving essential information on sales and other key information. The example on the following pages includes suggested information.

The majority of the information on this sample report has been extracted from till-generated data.

SAMPLE WEEKLY REPORT

Name: Any Charity   **Shop Details:** 27 High St, Anytown   **Week Ending:** May 13, 2006   **Week: #19**

INCOME	Calc	Sun £	Mon £	Tues £	Wed £	Thurs £	Fri £	Sat £	Week Total £	Items Sold	Av. Unit Selling Price
Sales											
Direct Donated Clothing			57.89	105.63	194.61	96.24	45.23	139.87	639.47	312	2.05
Direct Donated Non-Clothing			12.69	15.56	24.95	27.89	32.96	28.14	142.19	67	2.12
Collected Clothing			169.36	85.25	75.36	45.78	129.87	196.87	702.49	289	2.43
Collected Non-Clothing			32.01	23.69	21.87	21.36	18.79	11.06	128.78	102	1.26
Any Charity Ltd (new goods)								8.05	8.05		
Total Sales	A		271.95	230.13	316.79	191.27	226.85	383.99	1620.98		
Rag Income						129.00			129.00		
Cash Donations				10.00				5.00	15.00		
TOTAL INCOME	A		271.95	240.13	316.79	320.27	226.85	388.99	1764.98		
Expenditure											
Petty Cash Expenditure			0.46	24.99	10.57	7.98	0.46	4.12	48.58		
Refunds						3.95		1.95	5.90		
TOTAL EXPENDITURE	B		0.46	24.99	10.57	11.93	0.46	6.07	54.48		
TOTAL INCOME (less TOTAL EXP)	A-B=C		271.49	215.14	306.22	308.34	226.39	382.92	1710.50		
Total Banked	D		271.56	227.57	307.22	303.34	225.56	381.82	1717.07		
Bank slip number			96039	96040	96041	96042	96044	96045	96046		
Discrepancy	D-C		0.07	12.43	1.00	-5.00	-0.83	-1.10	6.57		

Comments

Poor day on Thursday due to torrential rain. Landlord's agent visited on Tues to inspect heating system - he will send his report to Any Charity Head Office.

SAMPLE WEEKLY REPORT- PART 2

Petty Cash Analysis

Date	Description	Cost £	Signature of Recipient
8	*Milk*	*0.46*	
9	*Kettle*	*19.99*	
9	*Window Cleaner*	*5.00*	
10	*Light bulbs etc.*	*10.57*	
11	*Vol. Expenses*	*7.98*	
12	*Milk*	*0.46*	
13	*Stamps*	*4.12*	
	Total	*48.58*	

Sales Statistics

Sales This Week	*1,621*
Sales Same Week Last Year	*1,506*
Average Weekly Sales - Year To Date	*1,603*
Target Sales This Week	*1,625*
Sales Year to Date This Year	*30,406*
Target Sales Year To Date	*32,000*
Sales Year to Date Last Year	*29,496*

Collection Sack Information

Sacks Distributed this week	*950*
Sacks Returned - Full	*187*
Sacks Returned - Empty	*260*
Remaining stocks - Boxes	*4*

Volunteer Information

Numbers recruited this week	*1*
Numbers lost this week	*2*
Total contingent	*17*
Estimated total hours worked this week	*43*

Declaration

I certify that the above is a true and accurate record of

the week's transactions

Signature ....

Print Name ....

Job Title ....

Dated

Scrutiny of the report will reveal useful management information and trigger off certain prompts for action:

Weekly Report Comments

Heading	Comments / Prompts for Action
Total sales by day	Saturday is the best trading day – do we have enough volunteer cover on that day? Not trading on Sunday - is it worth a try?
Analysis by department	Clothing (collected and direct donated) at £1,342 accounts for 83% of total sales – is it getting enough display space? Conversely, new goods returned only £8.05 – does it need replenishing or taking off?
Average Unit Selling Prices	How do these compare with other shops in the chain? Do we need to adjust? Very low AUSP on collected non-clothing – Investigate!
Petty Cash	Kettle at £19.99 – Seems expensive - £9.99 in Argos! – Investigate
Banking Discrepancies	Over £5.00 on Tuesday – What happened? Investigate
Bank slip number	Out of sequence - # 96043 missing!! Why? – Investigate
Collection Sack Info	19.6% response. Down to four boxes – Arrange delivery
Volunteer Info	Net decrease of one volunteer – Monitor
Sales Statistics	Ahead of LY but down on Target.
Declaration	A signed statement can be particularly useful during 'discrepancy' investigations.

A copy of the Weekly Report should be filed and kept in the shop as a reference to past performance and the origin of information for previous year required for the Weekly Report etc.

Banking

It is recommended that cashing up and banking is done daily with the minimum of cash kept on the premises. However, where there is a suitable fireproof safe on the premises and adequate insurance cover in place, banking can be less frequent.

The till drawer should be left open after the shop is shut – in the event of a break-in, this avoids the till being forced open and damaged.

If banking is done after bank hours, the cash can be placed in lodgement bags and deposited in a night safe or QuickSafe facility though there is usually a charge for this service. It is best to discuss with your bank which of their available options is the best match for your needs.

For reasons of personal safety, it is advised to vary the time and route taken to the bank and, where possible, two people should go, with one carrying the money and the other a personal alarm. **Staff and volunteers should never put themselves at risk.**

Sharing Information

Where two or more shops are run by a charity, it is a good idea to distribute a weekly information sheet or newsletter to all shops. Such sharing brings many benefits:

- Fosters feeling of 'team'.

- Spotlights to peers' sales performance, both good and poor. The former gives deserved recognition and hopefully, the latter gives a prompt to do better!

- Can be used to impart up-to-date news on the parent charity.

- An efficient way to disseminate shop-related instructions and suggestions.

Whilst many charities still communicate with their shops by surface mail, many have adopted instant communication via e-mail. One charity that did not have the budget for computers and printers etc. reverted to an older technology by installing fax machines in all shops arguing that not only were they cheaper than computers but were also simpler to use for their largely non computer-literate staff.

Overleaf is an example of a simple sales summary that could be incorporated into the suggested weekly newsletter:

Example Sales Summary

Any Charity

Weekly Sales Summary – w/e 13/05/06   Week 19

Shop	Week				Year to Date			
	Actual £	Bud-get £	Vari-ance %	Last Yr £	Actual £	Bud-get £	Vari-ance %	Last Yr £
Anytown	1,621	1,625	**-0.2**	1,506	30,406	32,000	-5.0	29,496
Anyville	2,003	1,895	+5.7	1,657	36,805	34,000	+8.2	27,405
Anycity	1,126	1,050	+7.2	1,360	18,963	17,500	+8.4	19,587
Total	**4,750**	**4,570**	**+3.9**	**4,523**	**86,174**	**83,500**	**+3.2**	**76,488**

Comments: A good week overall with the chain being ahead of budget and last year. Special congratulations to Anycity shop for returning the greatest growth on budget both for the week and year to date.

Record Books

Many charity shop chains have introduced a series of record books to their shops, designed to improve security. Their range and uses are described as follows:

Signing-In Book Example

Date	Name	Volunteer Staff Contractor Visitor	Time In	Time Out	Hours Worked	Signature

Uses:

- Maintains a record of who is in the shop at any point in time. In large, multi-floored shops this is vital information when evacuating a building following a fire alarm etc.

- Calculates voluntary hours worked (required for Weekly Report).

- Can be useful information during a security investigation to ascertain who was present at specific at specific times.

Staff and Volunteer Purchase Book Example

Date	Buyer's Name	Goods Bought	Full Retail Price	Price Paid	Receipt No.	Buyer's Signature	Man-ager's Signature

Uses:

Many charities offer staff and volunteers a discount on marked price with the transactions recorded formally. The level of discount is normally set at around 20% and is limited to a defined number of items per week and often restricted to items already priced and previously offered for sale at full price for a set period.

Goods Removed Book Example

General		Goods Removed				Goods Returned		
No. items	Descr-iption	Date out	Reason	Signature of person removing	Manager/ witness signature	Date In	Signature of person returning	Manager/ Witness Signature
4	Tops	18/ 06	Washing			25/ 06		
1	Brace-let	19/ 06	Repair			25/ 06		
1	Gent's watch	21/ 06	Valua-tion			30/ 06		

Uses:

There are many occasions when stock has to be removed from a shop for washing, repair or valuation etc. It is important that a record of its removal is kept and that the relevant manager checks to see that items are returned.

8

Shop Managers, Training and Volunteers

Paid Management

Most charity shops today are managed by salaried staff, though early shops were run entirely by volunteers and there are still a few shops which maintain the tradition. **For many chains, staff costs are the single largest operating expense accounting for an average of 28% of sales or an estimated £150m annually for the sector.**

To the uninformed this level of expenditure may seem unjustified and at odds with the traditional expectations of a charitable venture. However, the reality is that whilst a rota of willing volunteers may have been appropriate for the amateur shops of the 1960s and 1970s, today's longer-trading hours and more sophisticated shops require greater amounts of professionalism, time and application than would normally be available through volunteers.

Today charities will often invest tens of thousands of pounds to set up a shop as well as committing to annual outgoings of £50,000 or more. This is - by any standards - a sizable business for which the charity has a responsibility to protect its investment. This is best achieved by employing professional and consistent management, able to commit to a full working week, and where the employee is contractually obliged to fulfil the duties of the job description.

A further argument for paid management is that it usually allows longer trading hours. Shops run entirely by volunteers frequently trade for limited hours to fit in with particular domestic arrangements, often 10am-4pm for five days per week. This gives a total of 30 hours per week. Whereas, shops run by paid managers are usually open from 9am-5pm for six days per week.

This gives a total of 48 hours per week – a significant increase of 18 hours or plus 60%.

These extended hours attract extra sales, which are more often than not sufficient to cover the cost of salaried staff. What's more, the longer the shop is open the more stock donations it will attract and the more likely it is to trade during bank holidays and on worthwhile days between Christmas and New Year when many volunteer-run shops are understandably closed.

Finding the Manager

As has already been mentioned, a good manager is key to the success of any charity shop as she/he has more influence on sales than most shop managers would have in a commercial shop. It used to be said that the difference between a good and indifferent store manager at M&S was 1% of turnover since there was little scope to influence the range of merchandise, price, in-store promotion or staffing levels as these were already prescribed by head office. The 1% influence resulted from the manager's skill over convincing head office that his store should have first shipments of new lines or state-of-the-art display equipment etc.

In effect, many so-called 'managers' might be better described as 'caretakers' as they basically implement the company's store policy rather than 'managing' or influencing sales-generating aspects of their shop or store.

By contrast, the influence that a charity shop manager has on turnover is vast. Many charities have witnessed a huge variation in sales following a change to shop management – differences of plus or minus £500 p.w. are not unusual. On previous sales of £2,000 p.w. that is a variation of 25% and could mean plus or minus £25,000 p.a. on net contribution.

It follows that finding a good shop manager is essential. So what qualities and experience should we be looking for and where are we likely to find them?

Qualities Sought in a Good Manager

Essentially, we are looking for someone who genuinely wants to take on the wide-ranging responsibilities and hard work involved in

91

running a charity shop. Such tasks include stock generation, preparation and disposal, pricing, volunteer recruitment and motivation, promotion, cash handling, administration, and health and safety. Bizarrely, these onerous and extensive responsibilities are often willingly undertaken for a lower salary than would be offered to a supermarket checkout worker!

The fact that we do manage to recruit implies that money is not the 'be all and end all' for everyone. Happily, for many the chance to influence events or 'change the world' is a big attraction that is not offered by many jobs. In effect, running a charity shop is about as close to managing one's own business as you can get without risking personal finances.

For many there is the added attraction that the job exists to provide funds for a good cause rather than line the pockets of directors and shareholders etc. Though commendable, **empathy for the cause should not take precedence over relevant experience as the latter has a greater influence on the shop's profitability**, which is after all, the reason why it was set up in the first place.

These and other desirable and useful attributes for a prospective shop manager are summarised in the following table:

Qualities in a Shop Manager

Desirable	Useful
Enjoys challenge and responsibility – relishes scope for personal initiative	An affinity with the charity's cause
An excellent organiser	Previous retail experience preferably within women's fashion and/or charity retailing
A leader and motivator of people	An appreciation for the value of things
Likes to be kept busy; hard working	Numeracy and basic admin skills
Physically fit	Well-known and respected in the community – has contacts
Scrupulously honest	An artistic streak, e.g. flair for display

Whilst it would be a bonus to discover a manager with all the listed qualities, in the real world, these are seldom found and the recruiter usually has to compromise. In many ways selecting staff is akin to buying a house where certain requirements **must** be met, such as the number of bedrooms and proximity to shops and schools, whereas a double-garage and level garden might remain on a 'wish list' rather than a reality.

Advertising Options

So how do we go about finding a shop manager who meets all or most of the desired criteria? The main options are listed below:

Advertising for a Shop Manager

Method	Comments
Local Press Advertisement	This is how most such jobs are advertised – advertising copy should stress the challenging nature of the job and the scope for personal initiative etc. Hopefully this will attract people with the entrepreneurial skill we are seeking.
Job Centres	These can be effective and have the advantage of being free. Additionally, Job Centres often lend a room for interviews.
Internal Vacancies Bulletin	Larger charities may distribute such bulletins in hard copy and/or via e-mail. Many successful shop managers have evolved from seemingly unrelated jobs such as admin and hands-on care staff. For charities with an established chain of shops the obvious promotion route is from shop volunteer or paid assistant manager.
Shop Window	Perhaps the most obvious and effective but often overlooked. It's free, can be as large as you want and likely to be seen by people who live in close proximity to the shop. Remember to state that the job is a paid position, as many will wrongly assume that all charity shop jobs are voluntary.

Sadly, not all attempts at advertising yield the right calibre of applicant. **Too often 'second best' applicants are appointed, especially when there is pressure to get a new shop opened**

or keep an existing shop trading. Because getting the right manager has such a dramatic effect on sales and profitability, it is best to re-advertise despite the fact that the shop may remain closed for a further period. The old adage "act in haste, regret at leisure" is particularly apt here!

Induction and Probationary Period

Once a suitable manager has been appointed it is important that she/he receives a relevant and well–planned induction. This should include background information on the charity's purpose and ideals, guidance on Health and Safety requirements and, of course, operating procedures for the shop. Charities running a chain of shops often second an established shop manager to show the new recruit the ropes or place the new manager in another of the charity's shops for initial training.

Most charities operate a probationary period for new staff, which is normally three or six months from the date of joining. It is essential that the new manager is carefully supported and monitored during this period with every effort made to ensure success in the new job. However, where it is evident that, despite the support and effort of all concerned, the new shop manager is not "up to the job" then the employment should be terminated before the expiry of the probationary period or the probationary period should be extended pending further review. As harsh as it may seem, there is no point in tolerating an ineffective shop manager – it is not fair to the charity and often not fair to the employee.

By contrast, a long-serving and effective shop manager is worth their proverbial weight in gold. Some charities make phenomenal profits from indifferently located shops due largely to the dedication, business acumen and popularity of a unique and inspirational manager. Such managers should be treasured and appreciated – or to quote from South Pacific's *Some Enchanted Evening*; "Once you have found her, never let her go!"

Regular surveys of recruitment methods used, salary levels and other employment-related topics are covered in the Association of Charity Shops' Members' Handbook.

Shop Managers' Training

Whilst running charity shops 20 years ago would have been regarded as a largely uncomplicated and amateur operation, today's higher investment, legal requirements and the more refined techniques used have made it a more complex and sophisticated fundraising enterprise. The sector can no longer rely solely on the common sense approach of enthusiastic amateurs.

Many of the large "hundred-plus" charity shop chains have employed specialist trainers to support their shop managers and assistants etc. This is a luxury not afforded to smaller charities running just a handful of shops. Nevertheless, relevant training should be given, some of which can be organised in-house and some externally.

The following table may be useful in suggesting the topics to be covered and how provided:

Staff Training Suggestions

Training Topic	Delivered	
	In-house	**Externally**
History, Work and Aspirations Of Parent Charity	Essential and motivating background information for all employees	
Responsibilities under Health and Safety Act	With reference to the Association of Charity Shops' guidance in their Members' Handbook and Training Video	An external speaker can be used; also training workshops from Association of Charity Shops
Responsibilities under the Disability Discrimination Act (DDA)	With reference to the Association of Charity Shops guidance in their Members' Handbook	An external speaker can be used
Shop theft, Challenging Behavior, Card Fraud, and CHIP and PIN (5 videos)	Relevant videos can be borrowed from the Association of Charity Shops and further guidance in its Members' Handbook	An external speaker can be used; also training workshops from Association of Charity Shops

Training Topic	Delivered	
(continued)	In-house	Externally
Spotting and Valuing Antiques and Collectables	Video on Dating Ceramics available from Association of Charity Shops	Often a local auction house will provide a representative to present this training
Stock Generation and preparation, Shop Layout, Pricing, Shop Administration, Volunteer Recruitment and Motivation	Training on these topics can be given in-house by reference to the relevant sections in this guide	The Association of Charity Shops can be approached to recommend a trainer to speak on one or more of these topics

Shop Volunteers

Shop volunteers are the lifeblood of charity shops. Without their willingness to offer time and effort, the sector would cease to be a viable fundraising activity. If costed at just the minimum wage, the millions of hours given annually to serve, sort, hang, steam and cull stock etc., would exceed the total net profit generated from all the shops operating in the UK. In other words, **without volunteers, the sector could not continue as it could not afford to pay for the labour currently provided free by volunteers.**

Many and Various

Volunteers' ages, backgrounds and reasons for volunteering are many and various. They may range from a teenager anxious to gain work experience to a recently widowed seventy-year-old wanting a reason to get out of the house to meet new people and do something worthwhile. They might even be a convicted drunk-driver serving out a community service order.

One charity shop chain manager tells of meeting an elderly volunteer in Bradford who, as a young woman of eighteen, packed shells for the Great War and would write flirtatious messages to the troops on the shell cases! Another volunteering in a shop at Kilburn recalled the time when she had been a housemaid for

Edward, The Prince of Wales and Wallace Simpson. Despite being severely pressed by the other volunteers for titbits of information, she remained steadfastly loyal to her former employees by not betraying any "Royal secrets"!

Appreciating Volunteers

Given that they are such a vital ingredient, volunteers are not always appreciated. One male volunteer in his late sixties complained of the fact that whenever his shop received a visit from the area manager, she would sail past him with a perfunctory acknowledgement and head for the manager to discuss ways and means to resolve current performance problems. The volunteer wished he too had been consulted as he could have offered so much – after all, he was a retired management consultant, but no one had bothered to find that out!

Employing an external facilitator, one charity organised a brainstorming session aimed at finding ways to increase profit. To prove a point the facilitator asked detailed questions about the Christmas card business in shops – "What were your overall sales?", "What was the best selling design?", "How many packs remain unsold?" The relevant manager was able to answer all the questions correctly.

The facilitator then posed similar questions concerning volunteers – "How many do you have?", "How many have you lost in the last year?", "What were their main reason for volunteering?", "How many do you have under twenty-five years of age?" Sadly, managers were not able to provide the answers here. The facilitator responded by asking what was more important for the business; Christmas cards or shop volunteers? His point was well made and a salutary lesson learned.

Numbers Required

The absolute minimum requirement for a shop is just one volunteer present at all times. For a relatively busy shop, having three or four present would be desirable with, for example, one or two deployed on the sales floor with two or three processing stock in the stockroom.

Based on the results of one charity's research where they gave an average of one and a half days per week, we can roughly calculate that a rota of 16 volunteers would be required to ensure four being present at all times. Based on a multi-charity survey taken in 2004 the average number of volunteers per shop was 19.

Diversity

The accepted profile of the archetypal charity shop volunteer is female, white, middle class and over 50 years of age. Whilst we suspect that this profile still represents the majority of volunteers, many charities are attempting to attract volunteers from a wider spectrum of the community - in particular, younger people, men, people from ethnic minorities and those with a disability.

In an attempt to attract greater diversity, one charity designed a range of recruitment posters depicting images of people of all ages and backgrounds deployed in a variety of shop volunteer tasks. Others have had success by placing advertisements and editorial in local minority group publications.

Like so many sectors of society, people of similar backgrounds often tend to flock together feeling more comfortable in the company of like-minded people. People on the 'outside' are often made to feel uncomfortable and unwelcome and as such cease to volunteer. One charity tells of a teenage girl volunteer who left after just a week as she was fed up with the unwanted advice she received daily from what she described as all the "interfering mum substitutes"!

It is regrettable when bigoted attitudes prevail in charity shops - unlike many special interest groups, our shops and the people who work in them should be fully representative of their local community.

Finding Volunteers

People's reasons for volunteering their time can be widely varied. A few are detailed overleaf:

Volunteering Motivations

Influence/Motivation	Comment
Responded to a window poster appeal	For most charities volunteer recruitment posters should be a constant feature of the shop's window
Was approached by the manager whilst a customer in the shop	Often a productive approach though seldom used
As a result of a web search for volunteering opportunities	An increasingly popular way to research possibilities
Strong affinity with charity's cause – usually a hospice or medical research charity	Often following a loved-one's bereavement
Attended - and was motivated - by a recruitment event	Some charities run recruitment days where prospective volunteers are invited to the shop for a presentation on the work of the charity
Referred by a volunteer bureau or government volunteering programme	
Placement as part of a job experience initiative	Charity shops placements are a popular choice for both organisers and clients
Placement as part of a community service programme	These are unthreatening individuals such as driving offenders etc.
A direct approach from the manager or an existing volunteer being a friend or relation	Although not quantified, it is suspected that this approach brings many new volunteers

A common feature of a very successful charity shop is an above-average number of volunteers working as a happy and fulfilled team. Teams of 50 and more are not unusual. For many volunteers the shop forms an important part of their life where, as well as gaining satisfaction from doing something worthwhile, they benefit from the companionship and fun times enjoyed amongst friends.

A happy and well-managed shop will quickly get a reputation as good place at which to volunteer and so attract yet more volunteers – a proven case of "success breeding success" and due again in no small part to the influence and reputation of that most valuable of assets – the shop manager.

To recognise the contribution of shop volunteers many charities distribute individual awards for long service or group awards for particularly effective shop teams. At one such presentation ceremony for long-service awards, one charity manager thanked a volunteer profusely for her long and dedicated service, and was gratified to receive the response; "No, I should be thanking you as without the shop and the friends I meet my life would be a lot duller!" It is a heart-warming example of a true win-win situation.

A number of organisations offer information and advice on volunteering and volunteer management – see the Useful Information and Further Contacts *section of this guide.*

9

Marketing, Advertising and Promotion

One of the many textbook definitions for *Marketing* is: "The process of communicating with a specific market to offer goods or services for sale".

Following this definition, charity shops provide a unique opportunity to communicate the charity's cause. Yet, sadly and all too frequently, customers are unaware of the charity supported by the shop they are in, often referring to it as the "Oxfam shop!" where Oxfam has become the generic term for a charity shop á la *Hoover* and *Biro!* For example, one charity recalls the day it received a call from a regional TV news programme to say that it wanted to film in one of the charity's city-centre shops – the news item was to feature a family affected by unemployment and its need to buy second-hand clothing. The mother duly spoke to camera praising the helpful service received and the bargains bought saying that: "Nowadays we have to come down the Oxfam to get our stuff." In fact, the shop was not Oxfam at all but a leading *disability* charity that was hoping to benefit from some free publicity!

Similarly, for many charity shops the branding on the outside of a shop is often weak with only a small proportion of the fascia area used to promote the charity.

A charity shop offers a <u>cost-free</u> opportunity to advertise its cause, its products, its special offers and its benefits.

This is a big advantage as, by contrast, paid advertising can be expensive – a quarter page advertisement in a national paper can start from £15,000 and even £1,000 - £2,000 in regional papers. Leaflets can cost hundreds of pounds to print and deliver and poster sites at bus stops can be several hundreds of pounds.

Despite such expenditure a charity cannot always be certain that the advertising is reaching the right people to prompt the awareness and support intended. As well as promoting the cause, charity shops with their high street presence are ideally placed to appeal for those two essential ingredients of their business - stock donations and volunteers.

Text should be of a size that can be read clearly from a distance, so keep slogans punchy. And if there is a 'call to action' (donations, volunteers, websites) make sure these are also clearly displayed.

To ensure effective communication with customers and passers-by, charities must make sure that all media is professionally designed with simple and clear messages thoughtfully displayed for maximum impact. Striking images and photographs will capture public's attention - but be careful not to use too strong an image that may upset or offend.

During the late 1980s the RSPCA ran a harrowing press advertisement depicting a huge pile of dead dogs. Though this advertisement alerted the attention of an entire nation to the plight of abandoned dogs, it caused distress to many. A less offensive, though effective poster campaign run by a national charity for the disabled depicted an image of a wheelchair-user outside a public convenience accessed via a steep staircase. The copy ran: "This is neither public nor convenient". Similarly, this charity also produced a poster showing a car illegally parked in a 'disabled only' parking bay, where the clever copy ran: "Is this the only time you put yourself in our place?"

Design and Branding

For designing and printing, use the most professional service you can. Nothing pollutes the otherwise professional image of a charity shop more than scrawly hand-written posters – these should be avoided. Remember you are a professional retail operation! Larger charities may use an 'in-house' design service but if this is not available then enquire of your staff to see whether they have any contacts with sympathetic graphic designers. Some charities have successfully approached their corporate supporters for *pro bono* design services.

Failing that, some very effective graphics can be created on home PCs by scanning in photos and adding text and then having them printed off at local copy shops – or maybe a volunteer has a creative flair.

Take time to look at other retail shops - including charity shops - to see how they use promotional materials to attract attention to their stock. Look to bring seasonal trends and designs into shops by reflecting the colours of a season in eye-catching posters or rail-mounted cards. Follow the theme of your window display through to the inside of the shop with small displays of coordinating stock at special focal points throughout the shop. Furthermore, don't just stick to seasonal promotions; look to other events for inspiration, such as Easter, Valentine's Day, Halloween, St George's, St Andrew's and St Patrick's Day, plus local village/town fête days. All of these can be combined to create themed promotions within a shop and keep the customer interested.

The use of consistent branding is essential throughout all promotional materials, be it campaign posters, sales promotion materials or leaflets. There should be a clear use of the charity logo, with the wording and tone of message fitting with the charity – make sure you consult and take advice from appropriate departments within your charity to ensure that any creative materials you produce fit within agreed guidelines.

Posters and Leaflets

Plan your promotional materials to fit with your shops – look at the space available to you and utilise 'dead' space. One frequently under-used area within a shop is the area above the wall rails to the ceiling – typically there will be a gap of between one and three feet in which to place eye-catching images or messages promoting your charity's work – keep them simple following the clean-cut branding. More wordy posters can be used in areas where customers will have time to stand and read – behind the counter for instance.

Posters displayed in the shop window should be of a professional standard. Avoid *Blu Tack*, which not only looks unsightly but also has limited hold when exposed to heat and light. Ensure that posters are hung vertically, do not obstruct the window display and are up-to-date giving current information. Too many charity shops plaster their windows with an untidy array of uncoordinated notices and posters ranging from "wedding dresses in stock" to a flyer advertising that the circus is in town. Try to limit the material to only the most essential.

Information leaflets can be placed on the counter top for customers to pick up – or, if your charity is promoting a particular campaign, consider placing leaflets in carrier bags. Some charities allocate an area of the shop as an information centre using a one-metre run of shelved space or custom-made leaflet holders affixed to the wall.

Price Tickets

Despite the fact that a typical charity shops will use 40,000 price tickets per year, not all shops use this largely cost-free additional advertising opportunity. Some do not even brand with the charity's name and many fail to use the reverse for printing stock and volunteer appeals plus key facts about the charity and contact 'phone numbers etc. Similarly, till receipts are often left un-branded – another lost opportunity!

Carrier Bags

In the early days, most charities would bag purchases in an assortment of donated carrier bags branded from Asda to WH Smith. Though incurring additional costs, branded carrier bags are now the norm, with charities recognising the benefits of continued advertising once the customer and the bag have left the shop.

It is interesting that branded bags were not always accepted. One national charity recalls the day way back in 1973 when it first introduced a branded bag only to find that the first and many subsequent customers coolly removed the contents and then turned the bag inside out before putting them back. The cruel reality was that customers did not want to advertise the fact that they had been shopping in a charity shop! Fortunately, nowadays the stigma attached to buying from charity shops has all but disappeared with customers proud to advertise the origin of their bargain purchases.

Stock Collection Sacks

It is also worth considering not only charity-branding your house-to-house collection sacks, but also using the available print area to appeal for shop volunteers and/or particular donated items. Alternatively, arrange for your sack supplier to insert a one-off, time-limited appeals leaflet into the envelope.

In order for any of these communications to have the best impact you must make sure that your staff are also well informed of the charity's work and especially on any current campaigns. There is no point getting the customer fired up about the charity's work only to have the enthusiasm curtailed by a negative or ill-informed member of staff.

The many charities who are members of the Association of Charity Shops and who have signed up to the *Code of Charity Retailing* may also include on their sacks the *Code of Charity Retailing* logo. The Code has been designed to promote high standards of charity retailing amongst participating members and to increase public confidence and support for charity shops.

Having a Clear Policy

Although the shop presents a valuable opportunity to promote your charity's name and work, it is important that it does not take precedence over what is normally the core purpose of the shop - to raise maximum funds! For instance, there may be pressure from the parent charity to allocate a substantial proportion of sales footage to an information-centre or even, where appropriate, a counselling or other similar service provided by the charity. Obviously, such a sacrifice of potential sales footage will diminish sales and the parent charity should make clear its overriding policy - is it to use its shops to raise maximum funds or to sacrifice profit in furtherance of its public awareness and service provision?

For one charity, where the shops were the responsibility of county-based independent groups, the policy was confusing, with some groups hell-bent on maximising profits and others justifying low profits or even trading losses by arguing that the provision of *free* clothing to needy individuals was in furtherance of its charitable objectives! All very confusing and frustrating for the manager with overall responsibility for the shops.

Sales Promotions

Another way to attract customers and sell more stock is the use of sales promotions – take ideas from the high street and adapt to fit with your shops. Seasonal sales are the most obvious – selling coats and jumpers in summer and excess shorts and t-shirts in winter. Set up clearly marked 'Sale' rails to attract customers – '3-4-2' and BOGOF (Buy One, Get One Free) are popular and effective promotions. However, remember that storage space permitting, it may be better to put aside unseasonable stock and bring it out again the following season when it can be ticketed at full price.

With any sale stock make sure it is very clearly priced and marked as 'sale' stock as opportunist customers may try to buy 'full-value' stock at sale prices. Always use professional signage for your promotions printed in-house or acquired from shopfitting companies.

Fascias and Decals

Shop fascias or signboards are a permanent, cost-free and effective way to promote the charity that the shop supports. An effective fascia uses the space available to full advantage by having the charity's name written bold and large, including a telephone number (useful for attracting house-collected donations), and including the road/street number.

Many charity shop fascias fall short by utilising only a small proportion of the available 'free' space. Moreover, where more than one shop is operated, the fascia design should be consistent across the chain – this gives an instant quality branding that shows the customer you are a professional retail operation.

Many charity shops also repeat their charity's name and logo on a decal affixed to the shop window either low down or at eye-level. Decals are effective at reinforcing the brand at close quarters i.e. where a customer is looking at a window display where the fascia is not visible.

Some charities also use window decals to convey key facts such as:

Last year *Any Charity*
• Funded 10,000 hospital beds
• Spent £10m on medical research
• Saved 10,000 lives
• Re-united 5,000 families

Opening Hours

Ensure that the shop's opening hours are clearly displayed on the door and a reminder that donations should not be left on the pavement outside these hours. Piles of black sacks left outside shops are invariably ransacked, causing an unsightly mess and a hazard for pedestrians.

It is particularly annoying when the residue of a jumble sale is dumped outside the shop after closing on a Saturday. Often this consists mainly of broken toys, indifferent bric-a-brac and dog-eared yellowing paperbacks – all unsaleable and costly to have cleared by the local council.

Websites

Today most charities have set up dedicated websites with this form of communication being increasingly used to impart information and generate funds etc. Where charities run one or more shops, it is important that their website includes information on shop addresses, trading hours, telephone number as well as an appeal for donations and volunteers etc.

Online Auctions

Due to the increasing popularity of online auction sites, many charity shops are now actively advertising some of their more interesting and collectable stock this way. It makes sense as an item displayed on, for instance, eBay has a potential 'world' market compared with the somewhat restricted market of the high street charity shop.

Some charities have set up a separate department to handle the process whilst others have contracted the work to an independent specialist who markets the items on behalf of the charity in return for a sales-related fee.

Whatever method is used, it is important to ensure that proper records are kept so that all transactions can be monitored and can be fully audited. Accordingly, it is recommended that your charity's accountant or Finance Department be consulted on setting up acceptable control procedures.

It is worth recording that one large charity who tested online auction selling commented that, although its shops were receiving higher prices for the items auctioned, without the more interesting bric-a-brac and books to display, they were losing some of their former customers for whom the shops were no longer the treasure trove they once were.

Public Relations (PR)

Public Relations is about creating and maintaining goodwill and understanding between a company and its public. For a charity shop this can have tremendous benefits. Like in-shop advertising and promotion, **Public Relations coverage is usually free.**

So who are your charity's 'publics' with whom you should communicate? The key groups an be identified as your customers, your donors, potential volunteers, current staff and volunteers, the local community and the general public as a whole.

The key part of PR is media relations – becoming friends with your local media – be it local newspapers, local radio or even regional TV. Find out the best contacts in all of these areas and start talking to them. Charity shops are full of interesting stories! Anything from unusual or valuable donations, to heart-warming stories about your volunteers, events, promotions or particular campaigns – all of these will make great stories for local press or radio. Take photos to send in with your letters and encourage journalists to come along to the shop to take their own photos or interview volunteers and staff.

Also use local media to appeal for new volunteers and stock donations – by combining this with a story surrounding your shop you can gain good press coverage without paying for advertising space.

New shops or re-openings also make good coverage – especially if you can get a local dignitary or minor celebrity to be involved in the opening – invite press and photographers along to make the most impact.

Writing the Press Release

- Collate and organise your facts. A simple rule is to find answers to the questions who, what, when, where, why, and how. Put a date on the release and remember, yesterday's news is old news.

- Create a catchy headline. Keep the headline short and simple using less than 10 words. It should convey the key point raised in the opening paragraph in a light-hearted manner that catches the imagination and attention. Follow on with the details of the story.

- Write in the 'Third-Person' tense. A press release must be presented objectively from a third person's point of view. Remove "you", "I", "we" and "us" and replace them with "he/she" and "they". Provide references for any statistics, facts and figures raised in the press release and refrain from expressing personal opinions, unless they are done in quotes.

- Provide "Quotes" from an appropriate person. Put the most important message down into a quote. It can make a story more 'real' if it can be backed up by an opinion or emotion.

- Provide additional background information if you can about the charity or particular campaign as well as who to contact for further information.

The above writing tips are not meant to be a complete guide to writing a good press release. But, should help you get started on writing a press release yourself.

Appendix C is a sample press release related to a charity shop topic.

Any Charity

1st June 2006

Press Release

(For Immediate Release)

Found at Last!

For years Doris Grimwood had been searching in vain to find a replacement dinner plate for the one she broke on Christmas Day 1966 while washing up after Christmas dinner! "I'd probably had a little too much to drink!", said Doris. It was part of a cherished dinner service, which was a very special wedding present from Doris' workmates when she married husband Ken way back in 1958.

After tracking down the manufacturers in Stoke-on-Trent, Doris was told that the pattern was out of production and that the only hope of finding one would be at a car boot sale, jumble sale or charity shop. That was 40 years ago and ever since then she has been rummaging through countless cardboard boxes at church hall bazaars, car boot sales and along the bric-a-brac shelves in hundreds of charity shops.

Imagine her surprise and delight when the very plate she had been seeking for all those years turned up in the *Any Charity* charity shop in Corporation Street, Anytown. "I couldn't believe it" said Doris, "I'd almost given up hope of ever finding one and there it was under a pile of other plates – I recognised the distinctive green and gold banding immediately and what's more it was in perfect condition without a chip or crack" Doris was so delighted with her find that she 'phoned husband Ken immediately and paid the shop £2 above the asking price of 45p.

Shop manager, Sylvia Hargreaves said she was always thrilled when customers found exactly what they were looking for. "It just goes to prove what unusual things you can find in charity shops and all at such bargain prices", Sylvia said.

The *Any Charity* shop in Corporation Street raises funds to support [*charity's cause*] and is one of seven shops in the area which contributed an amazing £123,000 last year. Sylvia is always on the look out for stock donations, new customers and volunteers. The shop can be contacted on tel: 0123 45678.

Contact Details
For more information contact [*name, telephone number and e-mail*]
Office Hours - 9.00-5.00 (Mon-Fri)

[Photo Enclosed]

10

Purchased Goods

Today many charity shops, selling predominantly used goods, supplement their stocks of donated items with a range of new merchandise purchased from independent suppliers – these are often referred to as 'bought-in-goods' to differentiate them from new goods that might have been donated. Specialist shops such as those run by museums and art galleries and particularly The National Trust sell entirely new goods.

Supporting the Cause

Most conventional charity shops sell purchased goods to increase overall sales and profit, although a minority stock them in furtherance of their charitable objectives. For example, a charity established to provide aid to underdeveloped countries might purchase and sell supplies of coffee, tea and craftwork, so providing an outlet for local production. The reasoning here is that it is better to provide funds for investment in a sustainable income-producing initiative than to give a one-off emergency donation – in other words, "better to give a man a fishing net than a fish".

Similarly, some charities running sheltered workshops etc. for people with disabilities might take a proportion of the craftwear production for sale in their shops. In these situations the charity is using its shops not solely as profit makers (as some potential profit may be lost) but partly as an extension of its *raison d'être*.

For the majority of charity shops, however, new goods are sold to increase profit. Like many aspects of charity retailing, there are differing opinions about the extent to which charity shops should be involved, with some arguing that unless they directly support the charity's cause, selling new goods is not recommended.

The table on the following page puts forward the significant arguments and issues.

The Pros and Cons for Selling New Goods

Pros	Cons
Bring additional sales and profit as well as adding interest and variety.	Compared with donated goods, they are time-consuming and complicated to administer. Require VAT returns, stock-takes, order placements. Suffer stock losses and breakages etc. Unless staff and volunteers are properly monitored, sales are not always properly recorded.
Attract new customers who are not conventional used-goods buyers. These customers may convert to donated-goods buyers, stock donators and volunteers.	Has to be administered through a separate trading company, as charities are not allowed to trade except in 'primary purpose' goods e.g. physical aids for the disabled. Profits are paid over to the parent charity using Gift Aid thus avoiding tax.
Particularly beneficial for supplementing Christmas trade when sales of donated stock are generally depressed.	Extensive involvement often upsets local traders who claim unfair competition as charities benefit from rate relief and low staff costs. Has been a major gripe of *The Federation of Small Businesses*.
Unlike the haphazard inflow of donated stock, defined products and quantities can be ordered.	Not in the 'spirit' of charity retailing as it does not exploit the sector's unique advantage of being able to attract donated stock. Why pay for it? Increases competition as any commercial shop can trade in new goods and are often better equipped to trade successfully.
By stocking lines already featured in a charity's Christmas catalogue, additional sales can be made; also a useful means of clearing end-of-season catalogue lines.	Could jeopardise qualification for rates relief as entitlement is subject to the premises being used for 'wholly or mainly' charitable purposes – hence, where new goods represent the major part of a shop's sales and/or display area, entitlement may be lost.
Customers expect to find a range of charity-branded Christmas cards on sale – it is a recognised and welcome feature of the traditional charity shop.	Higher than average stock losses can occur when 'unaware' shop volunteers are not sufficiently vigilant on the sales floor or when stock is not displayed securely.

Other Considerations

Undoubtedly, many of the large charity shop chains make substantial profits from selling new goods. However, it is a more costly, risky and time-consuming business than attracting and selling donated stock.

Some argue that the time, effort and money spent on sourcing and administrating new goods could be more profitably applied to generating more donated goods. For instance, rather than a shop investing say, £1,000 in a range of gift lines that, assuming all sell, might yield a profit of between £1,000 and £1,500, might it not be better to spend that money on more bag drops, schools/place-of-work collections or an appeal to industry for unwanted stock. Generally the returns here are greater, less risky, less time-consuming and more in keeping with the ethos of traditional charity shop retailing – a basically simple operation where the processes are more easily understood and supported by volunteers.

One leading charity in Australia running a chain of 30 shops in Victoria had a handful of shops which sold entirely gift lines and greeting cards. They were the inspiration of well-meaning trustees who decreed that gift lines were a "much nicer" business than smelly old clothes and discarded bric-a-brac! Although these shops looked wonderful and enhanced the reputation of the charity, they were not nearly as profitable as the charity's "simpler to manage and lower overhead" conventional charity shops - they have now been converted and profits have increased.

Similarly, a charity in Northern Ireland ran a café staffed entirely by volunteers who would not only serve at table but also prepared the sandwiches and baked the cakes. Although the café was popular and sales were acceptable, the inherent overheads of food ingredients, wastage and electricity etc. produced only minimal profits. That too was converted to a conventional charity shop after which sales remained similar but running costs were reduced by half.

On a more positive note, one enterprising UK charity has opened a chain of shops selling exclusively greetings cards, which are believed to be trading successfully. Greetings cards have always been an acceptable and expected product in charity shops.

Compared with many other purchased lines, they offer a good margin of profit, are very productive in so far as they take up relatively little display space in relation to their sales value and, as basically a 'goodwill' product, enjoy a close empathy with a charity's cause. Maybe we will see an escalation in such charity-managed shops.

Calculating VAT, Mark-up and Margin

The majority of new goods sold by charity shops will be subject to VAT at the current standard rate of 17.5% - the relevant exceptions being children's clothes and all books for which the VAT rate is 0% (zero rated).

Most charity trading companies will be registered for VAT meaning that they can reclaim VAT. The following example demonstrates how VAT, margin and mark-up is calculated:

Calculating VAT

	Units	Cost per unit £	Total £	VAT @ 17.5% £	Total inc VAT £	Total per unit £
Purchase Input VAT	100	2.00	200.00	35.00	235.00	2.35
Sell Output VAT	100	5.00	500.00	87.50	578.50	5.87
Profit		3.00	300.00		352.50	3.52
Due to Customs & Excise				52.50*		
Final Profit			300.00	00.00	300.00	3.00

* Difference between VAT Input and Output

When calculating profits, businesses often refer to either 'margins' or 'mark-ups' which are expressed as percentages. In the above example these would be calculated as follows:

Mark-up: £300 x 100 = **150%**   **Margin:** £300 x 100 = **60%**
     £200   £500

User Clauses

All shop leases will contain a 'User Clause' which is a contractual provision within a lease, that specifies the use or uses to which a property may be put and those which are prohibited. Most retailers will want the user clause to be as wide as possible.

Take a bookshop as an example. If the user clause says that the tenant can only use the premises "as a shop for the sale of books", that not only prevents the tenant from selling items such as maps and DVDs, but it means that when he wants to leave in the middle of the lease term, he can't find a buyer unless it's another bookshop. So it should say "as a shop for the sale of books and/or for the sale of any other goods with the landlord's consent, which consent shall not be unreasonably withheld".

Hopefully, in most cases charities have negotiated a fairly open-ended clause but where they have a more restricted one, they should check to see that the new goods intended are permitted. Where this is not the case they should approach the landlord for an amendment. Sometimes a landlord will refuse to do this when he owns a number of shops in a parade and, for the protection of his other tenants, he is trying to prevent any duplication of trade.

New Clothing

Whilst most charities' new goods comprise gift-type products such as ceramics, glassware, framed prints and artificial flowers, some have taken the initiative to offer clothing lines. One charity offers a basic range of low-priced men's underwear and socks and women's underwear and tights – for reasons of hygiene these ranges would not be sold secondhand. Hence, operating primarily as a general clothing retailer, this charity is filling a gap in its clothing range.

Another charity, recognising that large sizes in women's clothing were always in demand but seldom in stock, considered commissioning an overseas manufacture to supply an exclusive range of large sizes for sale in selected shops.

Supporting Local Craftspeople

Sometimes charity shops will support local craftspeople by displaying and selling their creations. Typical products would be paintings, hand-made greetings cards and knitted toys and garments. The items are usually sold on a commission basis with the charity retaining a percentage of the sale price with the balance remitted to the originator. Whilst these sales add interest to the shop and foster a sense of community, charities should make sure that the return they are getting per square foot is greater than or equal to what they would get from conventional donated stock – otherwise there is no point in doing it. They must also ensure that proper records are kept and that advice on the VAT and insurance implications has been sought.

Trade Fairs

Where a charity has decided to stock and sell conventional gift-type lines, the best means of sourcing stock is to visit one of the many city-based giftware and fancy goods fairs. There will be hundreds of manufacturers and importers exhibiting at these fairs and the products on view will give an indication of what items are currently in vogue – like clothing, the giftware business is subject to the vagaries of fashion – be it solar-powered garden lights or magnetic dart boards. Try to find a supplier who will let you have stock on a sale or return basis. The mark-ups on giftware are generally high, typically ranging from 100% - 200%.

In Summary

Originally charity shops were set up solely for the receipt and sale of donated goods – a simple concept that exploits the sector's unique advantage in not having to buy stock.

Trading in new goods is inherently more risky and time-consuming than the simpler business of selling donated items where there is little paper work involved, no cost of sales and where the consequences of theft are less dire.

With the possible exception of greetings cards, new goods should only be considered where it is believed that additional profits will result and where the charity has sufficient resources in place to manage it properly.

Remember that charity shops are covered by the requirements of trading standards and consumer regulations, as well as the requirements of charity law regarding trading in purchased goods.

11

Management and Support

For small charities, the setting up of their first shop is usually a means to add income to an already established armory of traditional charitable appeals and is often the brainchild and responsibility of what is frequently the charity's sole fundraiser.

Once the fundraiser has established a handful of shops, a specialist shops manager is usually appointed to take overall responsibility for the chain. This is a sensible approach as today the management of charity shops is a specialist operation requiring retail experience and a more commercial management approach than would be appropriate for general fundraising.

A typical field management structure would be as follows:

Managing Shops of Differing Sizes

Chain Size	How Managed
Small	Often a locally-based charity where a handful of shops is managed by the fundraiser with the shops usually run by volunteers.
Medium	Usually a national charity with shops managed at a regional level by area fundraisers or specialist area retail manager/s using paid or voluntary shop managers.
Large	Invariably, a national charity with an established specialist retail department using dedicated regional retail managers and area retail managers. For example, a chain of say, 160 shops would normally have two regional retail managers managing four to eight area retail managers each who in turn would oversee 10 to 20 shops each. Such chains would usually have a paid shop manager in each shop. These chains make up the majority of shops in the sector.

Qualities Sought in Area and Regional Management

Successful area and regional shop managers have evolved from a wide spectrum of past experience. These may range from retired RAF Squadron Leaders to former commercial chain-store managers. Happily, there are also a few who have climbed through the ranks from shop volunteer, assistant shop manager, shop manager, area manager and finally regional manager.

The essential qualities sought in an effective area/regional manager may be summarised as follows:

- Business acumen
- Inspirational leadership
- Motivator of people
- Performance driven
- Basic knowledge of accounting and employment law
- Problem solver
- Flexible
- Thriving on personal initiative

Although many of the above qualities would be equally appropriate for a commercial chain, there are a few additional ones that are perhaps unique to our sector – these are:

- Diplomacy
- Patience
- Tolerance

For instance, managers who have joined the sector directly from a hard-nosed commercial retail environment may find it difficult to come to terms with a largely volunteer workforce who will not always "be told what to do" – and why should they? Volunteers sometimes have to be cajoled or won over and it is here that diplomacy is a useful quality.

Similarly, because running a chain of shops is not the overriding purpose of the charity, the needs of the shops - which are understandably the shop manager's main concern - are seldom the charity's first priority. Hence, heartfelt pleas for funding for re-fits, performance-related pay, new shops and EPOS systems etc. often go unnoticed or are regarded as low priority compared with more pressing core charity priorities. It is here that the qualities of patience and tolerance are particularly useful.

It is worth noting that managers who have gained their experience in the commercial retail sector may have left an environment where the total focus of the business was pure and simple retail, whereas the focus of their charity employer is likely to be health, medical research, overseas aid or animal welfare etc. Here the needs of the shops are secondary to the core work of the charity.

Happily however, the majority of charity chain managers who have transferred from a commercial environment quickly acclimatise to the different culture of the charity shop sector and enjoy long and fulfilled careers in this very special and rewarding area of retail.

Unique Support Requirements

As has already been mentioned in the section on *Property Acquisitions*, running a chain of charity shops puts extra demands on a charity's general support functions – in particular, finance, HR and legal/secretarial departments.

For wholly understandable reasons, the functions of these departments are more attuned to serve the operations of the charity rather than the specific requirements of an ancillary shops chain. This is often a frustration for retail managers who are sometimes obliged to conform to attitudes and systems that do not always gel with the often unique needs of a fast-moving and performance-driven shops operation more akin to a commercial undertaking.

For instance, the charity's systems of budgeting and financial reporting are often inappropriate for the effective monitoring and controlling of a retail chain. To combat this, the retail departments of larger chains will often set up their own management accounting systems reporting performance against their unique key performance indicators such as average weekly sales, costs as percentages of sales, average unit selling prices and customer spend and return on capital employed.

Similarly, problems often arise over the management of shops' staff, particularly in disciplinary situations where retail management wants to take a speedy and firm line in situations of blatant dishonesty whereas HR might advise a softer and more sympathetic approach. Additionally, some charities have encountered opposition when recommending, for instance, a performance-related-pay incentive to be awarded against pre-set sales and/or profit targets – such inducements being regarded as "too commercial" and out of sympathy with the charity's established way of doing things.

To overcome these problems, some of the larger charity chains have recruited specialist finance, HR, property and training staff who form part of a stand-alone retail department operating independently from a general fundraising or income generation division. A few charities have gone so far as to operate their shops within an independent trading division having its own board of directors/trustees. However, charities must ensure that they do not jeopardise their entitlement to Uniform Business Rate relief, as the benefit is the privilege of charities per se and not limited trading companies.

To put priorities in perspective, it is helpful to remember that charities do not exist to run shop chains – rather, the **shops are solely a means to raise money and profile to support the core work of the parent charity.**

One charity chain manager recalls the time when he was directed by his charity's trustees to issue essential clothing free-of-charge to asylum seekers and refugees in sympathy with the charity's humanitarian work. Although sympathising with the needs of his charity's dependants, he did not take kindly to the prospect of sacrificing sales and profit and he said as much. He was soon 'put in his place' by the charity's CEO and learnt a salutary lesson about what should be his real priorities!

Communication

All this may seem a little negative but the needs, aspirations and achievements of the staff and volunteers who work in charity shops versus those involved with a charity's service provision and administration will be better understood and appreciated if regular and effective communication is encouraged.

Chain managers should ensure that news and achievements concerning their shops are regularly communicated to the charity's senior managers and publication editors etc. Similarly, the initiatives and achievements of the parent charity's core work should be communicated to the shops via newsletters, shops' staff attendance at conferences and senior staff visits to shops etc.

One national charity with a large shops chain which was experiencing a 'conflict of interest' with its parent charity appointed a *Human Resources Retail Support Manager* whose role was to serve and implement the unique HR needs of its charity shops. This proved to be an extremely effective and productive post, particularly because, although funded by the shops division, it sat within the charity's HR department. This meant that the post-holder was able to communicate to HR colleagues the unique needs of the shops and at the same time gain an appreciation for the wider needs of the parent charity.

A particularly effective way to communicate is face-to-face - especially in our sector where some shops staff and volunteers feel that, being located away from their charity's service centres and offices, they seldom have goodwill visits from the charity's senior management and trustees. Charities should not under-estimate the value of such visits, which mean so much to staff and particularly those working in isolation. It is worth remembering that being recognised and appreciated ranks high in Maslow's famous hierarchy of human needs.

Shops Review Checklist

Whether it be a general fundraiser or dedicated area retail manager who has responsibility for a group of shops, it is important that she/he makes regular visits to the shops to ensure that everything is being properly managed in accordance with the procedures laid down. It is recommended that these visits are sometimes unannounced as prior warning will often provoke 'special efforts' to reflect the shop in a more favourable light than might be the norm.

Too often an area manager will pay only a cursory visit, simply enquiring if everything is all right without exhaustive probing and investigation. To help ensure that visits are thorough and revealing, it is useful to use a standardised checklist, which covers all aspects of shop management – this is common practice in the outside world and analogous to the dreaded Ofsted reports so feared by head teachers etc.

Appendix D is a suggested checklist format which charities can adapt to suit their particular needs. It will be noted that scores are awarded against each section with 60 points being the maximum obtainable. Scores from a previous check are recorded on the first page so that any improvement or reduction in standards can be noted. Conscientious managers will usually be eager to improve on a previous score and will take pride and satisfaction from it. There is also provision on the checklist to comment on specific items and to record required dates for action etc.

Any Charity Shop Review Checklist | Appendix D

Manager's Name [   ]

Shop [   ]   **Date** [   ]

Number of active shop volunteers	
Score from previous check	
Retail Square Footage (A)	
Items hanging (B)	
Average no. hanging items per sq. foot (B divided by A)	
Issues/actions from previous checklist have been implemented (please circle)	**Yes/No**

Section 1 - Shop Appearance

	Yes	No
1. Exterior of premises clean and well maintained		
2. All lighting working and interior lighting used to display merchandise effectively		
3. Effective window displays, set up using appropriate seasonal stock and display materials		
4. Posters and banners displayed and attached as per guidelines		
5. All products in window clearly ticketed and visible from outside: opening hours, charity registration number also displayed		
6. Shop layout optimises available footage and allows ease of customer access		
7. In-store merchandising and display standards maintained		
8. Housekeeping standards maintained		
9. In-store signage current and displayed according to guidelines		
10. Shop smells fresh		

SCORE (max. 10) [   ]

Number (1-10)	Comments	Action When

Section 2 - Administration and Security

	Yes	No
11. Paperwork filed, files labelled logically		
12. Stationery and carrier bags ordered to ensure stocks are not depleted		
13. Cash Donations processed, recorded and paperwork completed correctly		
14. Cash Reconciliation completed daily, discrepancies reported and sales sheets completed		
15. Banking completed daily, associated paperwork filed, relevant security measures taken		
16. Cash on premises and till keys securely kept		
17. Petty Cash issued according to procedure, reconciled daily		
18. Refund/over-ring report checked daily, refunds issued appropriately		
19. Receipt roll and audit roll in use, audit rolls stored securely		
20. Pavement and counter collection box secured, positioned in areas of high customer flow and emptied as per guidelines		
21. 'No sale' and 'all void' transactions signed by till operator with reasons recorded		
22. Weekly till check actioned and recorded on weekly sales sheet		
23. Weekly sales sheets completed correctly & copies sent in accordance with procedures		
24. Staff purchases processed and logged according to procedure		
25. 'Goods Removed' book used and goods logged in accordance with procedure		
26. Secure lockers provided and utilised for staff's personal belongings		
27. Keys logged and issued correctly, keyholders accurately recorded with police/area manager		
28. Signing-in book used by all staff and volunteers		
29. Completion of volunteer starters/ leavers paperwork		
30. Incidents reported to area manager or equivalent and relevant action taken		

SCORE (max. 20)

Number (11-30)	Comments	Action When

Section 3 - Staff and Volunteer Management

	Yes	No
31. All staff and volunteers aware of *Any Charity's* ideals and current work		
32. All staff and volunteers able to communicate local services offered		
33. Weekly volunteer rotas displayed and briefed to all team		
34. All team identifiable as *Any Charity* staff or volunteers		
35. Awareness and communication of weekly sales targets and shop performance		
36. All new volunteers given relevant training and printed material		
37. Handling, sorting and till procedures coached with all relevant staff & volunteers		
38. Volunteer expenses issued according to procedure		
39. Daily use of either trading diary or hand-over book to maintain consistency		
40. Distribution of incoming communications to team		

SCORE (max. 10)

Number (31-40)	Comments	Action When

Section 4 - Customer Care

	Yes	No
41. All customers greeted at tillpoint and thanked for purchase		
42. All donors thanked for donation, donations immediately transferred to stockroom		
43. Telephone calls answered and dealt with professionally		
44. All enquiries about *Any Charity's* services answered professionally and customers referred to appropriate contact		
45. Customer complaints dealt with professionally and promptly, advice sought as necessary		

SCORE (max. 5) [　　]

Number (41-45)	Comments	Action When

Section 5 - Stock Generation, Processing and Management

	Yes	No
46. Evidence of appropriate pricing policy and implementation		
47. Stock meets agreed standards of quality and presentation		
48. Stock on display appropriate for season		
49. All stock items ticketed and coded correctly		
50. All garments sized accurately		
51. Stock density meets agreed targets		
52. House-to-House collection activity sufficient for needs of shop		
53. House-to-House collection sacks ordered to ensure stocks are not depleted		
54. Evidence of House-to-House collection monitoring and evaluation		
55. Evidence of controlled and appropriate use of stock rotation		
56. Valuables identified, documented and processed in accordance with valuable goods procedure		
57. Sales of collected stock processed separately to meet legal requirements		
58. Rags appropriately separated, stored ready for despatch and collection supervised		
59. Prohibited goods list displayed and goods disposed of as per guidelines		
60. Stockroom organised efficiently to allow safe systems of stock processing		

SCORE (max. 15)

Number (46-60)	Comments	Action When

GENERAL COMMENTS

(please include any training needs identified, with relevant action)

TOTAL SCORE (maximum 60)

Shop Manager's signature _____

Area Manager's signature _____

12

Useful Information & Further Contacts

This book provides an outline of the key aspects of charity retailing necessary to enable you to set up and run an efficient and successful shop operation. There are many additional sources of specialist information and guidance, a number of which are listed below.

Association of Charity Shops

The Association of Charity Shops is the UK-wide umbrella body supporting and representing the charity retail sector. The Association's website is an invaluable resource for both the public and charities. An up-to-date list of commercial suppliers to the charity retail sector can also be found here.
www.charityshops.org.uk
email: mail@charityshops.org.uk
tel: 020 755 4470

Propress Steamers

Donated clothes are the core of most charity shop's profits. For over 20 years Propress has supplied its range of durable, effective, highly efficient and commercial clothes steamers to charity shops. Propress steamers revitalise and freshen all manner of clothes, quickly and easily removing creases for perfect presentation, to maximise your income. We provide extra support, demonstrations and training for new shops, Health & Safety guidance together with dedicated staff for fast-track service to charities.
www.propress.co.uk
email: info@propress.co.uk
tel: 020 8417 0660

PROPRESS®

"We love fabric"

Business Support

Chip and PIN
Covers the new chip and PIN technology.
www.chipandpin.co.uk

Crime Reduction
Tips on reducing retail crime.
www.crimereduction.gov.uk/
email: public.enquiries@homeoffice.gsi.gov.uk
tel: 020 7035 4747

Professionals for Free
Facilitating voluntary sector contact with free/subsidised professional services.
www.professionals4free.org.uk
email: nicki.della-porta@bitc.org.uk
tel: 020 7566 6611

Charity Regulation

The Charity Commission
The Commission's website, covering all aspects of charity law including trading.
www.charitycommission.gov.uk
email: enquiries@charitycommission.gsi.gov.uk
tel: 0845 3000 218

Government Departments

Department for Environment, Food and Rural Affairs (DEFRA)
Covers all aspects of waste and recycling.
www.defra.gov.uk/environment/waste
email: helpline@defra.gsi.gov.uk
tel: 0845 9335 577

Department Of Trade & Industry: Better Business Framework
Provides guidance on retail issues, inc. furniture flammability regulations.
http://www.dti.gov.uk/bbf/index.html
email: dti.enquiries@dti.gsi.gov.uk
tel: 020 7215 5000

Environment Agency (EA)
Government body responsible for the environment's protection.
www.environment-agency.gov.uk
email: enquiries@environment-agency.gov.uk
tel: 08708 506 506

Inland Revenue and Customs and Excise
Covers Tax and Customs & Excise regulations.
www.hmrc.gov.uk
email: charities@inlandrevenue.gov.uk
tel: 0845 010 9000 or Charities Helpline: 0845 302 023

The Law

ACAS
Covers employment law.
www.acas.org.uk
email: acas@eclogistics.co.uk
tel: 08457 47 47 47

Ask Cedric
Covers trading regulations relating to charity shops (inc. pricing, safety, Sunday trading, consumer complaints, etc.)
www.askcedric.org.uk/
email: cedric@cambridgeshire.gov.uk
tel: 0845 3030 666

Disability Rights Commission
Tips on improving disabled access.
www.drc-gb.org/businessandservices
email: query form on website
tel: 0845 7622 633

DTI Employment Relations Directorate
Covers all aspects of employment law.
www.dti.gov.uk/employment/
email: dti.enquiries@dti.gsi.gov.uk
tel: 020 7215 5000

Health and Safety
Covers Health and Safety law.
www.hse.gov.uk
email: hse.infoline@natbrit.com
tel: 0845 345 0055

Trading Standards
Covers consumer protection information.
www.tradingstandards.gov.uk

Recycling

Community Recycling Network (CRN)
The national re-use organisation for community-based, not-for-profit and co-operative waste management groups.
www.crn.org.uk
email: info@crn.org.uk
tel: 0117 942 0142

Furniture Recycling Network (FRN)
Promotes the re-use of household goods.
www.frn.org.uk
email: info@frn.org.uk
tel: 0117 954 3571

Textile Recycling Association (TRA)
Representing Textile/Shoe collectors.
www.textile-recycling.org.uk
email: info@textile-recycling.org.uk
tel: 0870 042 8276

Voluntary Sector Support And Information

The Charities Resource Network
Covers good practice for accounting, investment, auditing, human resources, IT, planning and management.
www.thecrn.org.uk
email: info@thecrn.org.uk
tel: 0845 345 3192

Directory of Social Change (DSC)
Publishes literature; runs training courses on voluntary organisation management.
www.dsc.org.uk
email: info@dsc.org.uk
tel: 08450 777 707

Institute of Fundraising (IOF)
Represents and supports fundraisers.
www.institute-of-fundraising.org.uk
email: enquiries@institute-of-fundraising.org.uk
tel: 020 7840 1000

National Council for Voluntary Organisations (NCVO)
Issues affecting voluntary organisations.
www.ncvo-vol.org.uk
email: ncvo@ncvo-vol.org.uk
tel: 020 7713 6161

Volunteering

CSV
The Community Service Volunteers site.
www.csv.org.uk
email: information@csv.org.uk
tel: 020 7278 6601

Volunteer Development Agency, Northern Ireland
Covers volunteering & volunteer management in Northern Ireland.
www.volunteering-ni.org
email: info@volunteering-ni.org
tel: 028 9023 6100

Volunteer Development Scotland
Covers volunteering & volunteer management in Scotland.
www.vds.org.uk
email: vds@vds.org.uk
tel: 01786 479 593

Volunteering England
Covers volunteering & volunteer management in England.
www.volunteering.org.uk
email: information@volunteeringengland.org
tel: 0845 305 6979

Wales Council for Voluntary Action
Covers volunteering & volunteer management in Wales.
www.wcva.org.uk
email: help@wcva.org.uk
tel: 0870 607 1666

INDEX

138